Primitivism
and
Decadence

Primitivism and Decadence

A Study of American Experimental Poetry

By Yvor Winters

ARROW EDITIONS   NEW YORK

Bra

Nov. 3. 1941

Copyright, 1937, by Yvor Winters

Manufactured in the United States of America

4-9724 f2
(4 6 2)

To

WILLIAM DINSMORE BRIGGS

with profound admiration and a very

deep sense of intellectual indebtedness

CONTENTS

NOTE

THE present book is the result of a study which began about 1920, continued in a relatively desultory manner until about 1929, and then was pushed systematically to a conclusion in 1934. Small revisions and improvements have been made since that time, but the work was then essentially complete; in fact the basic outlines were laid down as early as 1933 in final form, and were published in *The Hound and Horn* (Volume VI, number 3) of that year in a review of T. Sturge Moore. I give these dates in order not to be accused of derivation from certain volumes which have recently appeared, and which touch more or less casually upon subjects herein treated. This study originally began as a sympathetic elucidation of the methods of the Experimental poets; it developed of necessity into an elucidation of their short-comings.

I am definitely indebted to Allen Tate, for two or three general concepts which are important in the development of this work, though I first became acquainted with his writing about 1926; I have endeavored to indicate this debt in the text. I have wherever possible employed the terminology of Kenneth Burke, and have acknowledged it, in order to avoid the unnecessary multiplication of terms; my own analysis of rhetorical devices began, however, about as early as his own, and was dropped for a time while his continued, because it did not seem especially fruitful. My own analysis was resumed when I discovered the key to the ethical significance of rhetoric and the possibility of creating an æsthetic on such an analysis; my quarrel with Mr. Burke, which will appear fully in this volume, is precisely that he has failed to do this. Any careful reader of the present volume will become aware of a general indebtedness to the late Irving Babbitt, who seems to me one of the few great critics of recent years, in spite of tremendous errors and limitations. Babbitt's social views appear to me unsound and unrelated to his literary views except through the most superficial verbal connections; his analysis of literary principles appears to me to be gravely vitiated by an almost complete ignorance of the manner in which the moral intelligence actually gets into poetry. Babbitt was unable to create a functioning body for his morality, much as Burke has been unable to give the rhetorical body which he has created a living spirit.

My most considerable debt is to William Dinsmore Briggs of Stanford University. This debt is difficult to define and is even awkward to acknowledge, for Professor Briggs, through steadfastly refusing to publish his major work, makes it impossible for me to acknowledge the debt except in the most general terms and runs the risk of being made responsible for my errors as a result of the acknowledgment. The debt is general, for Professor Briggs is a specialist in Renaissance thought and scholarship and in the history of criticism, and is not a specialist either in lyrical poetry or in modern literature. The debt is none the less profound, and I wish to be on record to the effect that the acknowledgment of it is no mere academic courtesy. I am indebted to Professor Briggs incidentally for many valuable suggestions in regard to detail, as I am indebted also to Franck Schoell and to René Lalou, both of whom very kindly examined and criticized this work in its early and immature stages, and to J. V. Cunningham and to R. P. Blackmur.

I should mention the following publications. Late in 1923 I published in the small magazine called *Secession* certain *Notes on the Mechanics of the Image.* In the two years following I revised these notes, and I revised them again later, but have temporarily laid them aside, since their interest appears to be one purely of rhetoric. In 1929 I published a long essay in *The New American Caravan* entitled *The Extension and Reintegration of the Human Spirit,* which, though redundant and full of error, laid down some of the principles herein contained. In a collection of essays

xii

by various authors, entitled *The Critique of Humanism,* edited by C. Hartley Grattan, and published in 1930 by Brewer and Warren, I published an essay later to be ludicrously misrepresented by Mr. Max Eastman, who appears to have quoted from it without having read it and to have supplied his quotations with an imaginary context; this essay was entitled *Poetry, Morality, and Criticism,* and its first section is an earlier draft of the first essay in the present volume. Two essays published in *Poetry: A Magazine of Verse* should be mentioned: a review of Robinson Jeffers, which appeared in the issue for February of 1930, and which is embedded with few alterations in the second essay of the present volume, and a review of *The Bridge,* by Hart Crane, which appeared in the issue for June of the same year, and which first outlined in rough form some of the ideas to be developed in this volume. Book reviews published in *The Hound and Horn* during the years 1931 to 1934 inclusive were based upon the present analysis, after it was well on its way to completion or even completed: of these, the most important are a review of Robert Bridges, in Volume V, Number 2; a review of T. Sturge Moore, already mentioned, in Volume VI, Number 3; and a review of the *Oxford Book of 16th Century Verse,* Volume VI, Number 4.

THE MORALITY OF POETRY

BEFORE attempting to elucidate or to criticize a poetry so difficult and evasive as that of the best moderns, it would appear wise to summarize as clearly as possible those qualities for which one looks in a poem. We may say that a poem in the first place should offer us new perceptions, not only of the exterior universe, but of human experience as well; it should add, in other words, to what we have already seen. This is the elementary function for the reader. The corresponding function for the poet is a sharpening and training of his sensibilities; the very exigencies of the medium as he employs it in the act of perception should force him to the discovery of values which he never would have found without the convening of all the conditions of that particular act, conditions one or more of which will be the necessity of solving some particular difficulty such as the location of a rhyme or the perfection of a cadence without disturbance to the remainder of the poem. The poet who suffers from such difficulties instead of profiting by them is only in a rather rough sense a poet at all.

If, however, the difficulties of versification are a stimulant merely to the *poet,* the reader may argue that he finds them a hindrance to himself and that he prefers some writer of prose who appears to offer him as much with less trouble to all concerned. The answer to such a reader is that the appearance of equal richness in the writer of prose is necessarily deceptive.

For language is a kind of abstraction, even at its most concrete; such a word as "cat," for instance, is generic and not specific. Such a word becomes specific only in so far as it gets into some kind of experiential complex, which qualifies it and limits it,

1

which gives it, in short, a local habitation as well as a name. Such a complex is the poetic line or other unit, which, in turn, should be a functioning part of the larger complex, or poem. This is, I imagine, what Mallarmé should have had in mind when he demanded that the poetic line be a new word, not found in any dictionary, and partaking of the nature of incantation (that is, having the power to materialize, or perhaps it would be more accurate to say, *being,* a new experience.)[1]

---

[1] Stéphane Mallarmé: *Avant-Dire* du *Traité du Verbe,* par René Ghil. Giraud, 18 Rue Drouot, Paris. 1886. Actually, Mallarmé seems to have had more in mind, though he should have had no more, in my opinion. The margin of difference is the margin in which post-romantic theory has flourished and from which post-romantic poetry has sprung. I quote the entire curious passage:

"Un désir indéniable à l'époque est de séparer comme en vue d'attributions différentes, le double état de la parole, brut ou immédiate ici, là essentiel.

"Narrer, enseigner, même décrire, cela va et encore qu'à chacun suffirait peut-être, pour échanger toute pensée humaine, de prendre ou de mettre dans la main d'autrui en silence une pièce de monnaie, l'emploi élémentaire du discours dessert l'universel reportage dont, la Littérature exceptée, participe tout, entre les genres d'écrits contemporains.

"A quoi bon la merveille de transposer un fait de nature en sa presque disparition vibratoire selon le jeu de la parole cependant, si ce n'est pour qu'on émane, sans la gêne d'un proche ou concret rappel, la notion pure?

"Je dis: une fleur! et, hors de l'oubli où ma voix relègue aucun contour, en tant que quelque chose d'autre que les calices sus, musicalement se lève, idée rieuse ou altière, l'absente de tous bouquets.

"Au contraire d'une fonction de numéraire facile et représentatif, comme le traite d'abord la foule, le parler qui est, après tout, rêve et chant, retrouve chez le poète, par nécessité constitutive d'un art consacré aux fictions, sa virtualité.

"Le vers qui de plusieurs vocables refait un mot total, neuf, étranger à la langue et comme incantatoire, achève cet isolement de la parole: niant, d'un trait souverain, le hasard demeuré aux termes malgré l'artifice de leur retrempe alternée en le sens et la sonorité, et vous cause cette surprise de n'avoir ouï jamais tel fragment ordinaire d'élocution, en même temps que la réminiscence de l'objet nommé baigne dans une clairvoyante atmosphère."

This is in some respects an admirable summary, and is certainly important historically. The entire tendency of the passage is to encourage the elimination of the rational from poetry. One should observe the sequence: "narrer, enseigner, *même* decrire," as if description were more nearly poetic than the other activities. The word *essentiel,* at the end of the first paragraph is the crux of the whole passage. The critic says that words have an obvious (that is, a rational) meaning, and a fringe of feeling, which he chooses to call essential: if only one kind of content is essential, we are naturally inclined to try to eliminate the other, and we have in this confusion, which reappears spontaneously, and without any discernible indebtedness to Mallarmé, in each successive generation of post-romantic poets, the real basis for post-romantic obscurantism. The sound idea that a poem is more than its rational content is thus perverted and distorted.

2

The poem, to be perfect, should likewise be a new word in the same sense, a word of which the line, as we have defined it, is merely a syllable. Such a word is, of course, composed of much more than the sum of its words (as one normally uses the term) and its syntax. It is composed of an almost fluid complex, if the adjective and the noun are not too nearly contradictory, of relationships between words (in the normal sense of the term), a relationship involving rational content, cadences, rhymes, juxtapositions, literary and other connotations, inversions, and so on, almost indefinitely. These relationships, it should be obvious, extend the poet's vocabulary incalculably. They partake of the fluidity and unpredictability of experience and so provide a means of treating experience with precision and freedom. If the poet does not wish, as, actually, he seldom does, to reproduce a given experience with approximate exactitude, he can employ the experience as a basis for a new experience that will be just as real, in the sense of being specific, and perhaps more valuable.

Now verse is more valuable than prose in this process for the simple reasons that its rhythms are faster and more highly organized than are those of prose, and so lend themselves to a greater complexity and compression of relationship, and that the intensity of this convention renders possible a greater intensity of other desirable conventions, such as poetic language and devices of rhetoric. The writer of prose must substitute bulk for this kind of intensity; he must define his experience ordinarily by giving all of its past history, the narrative logic leading up to it, whereas the experiential relations given in a good lyric poem, though specific in themselves, are applicable without alteration to a good many past histories. In this sense, the lyric is general as well as specific; in fact, this quality of transferable or generalized experience might be regarded as the defining quality of lyrical poetry.

What I have just said should make plain the difficulty of comprehending a poem exactly and fully; its total intention may be very different from its paraphrasable, or purely logical content. If

3

one take, for example, Mr. Allen Tate's sonnet, *The Subway,* and translate it into good scholarly prose, using nothing but the rational content of the poem as a reference, one will find the author saying that as a result of his ideas and of his metropolitan environment, he is going mad. Now as a matter of fact, the poem says nothing of the sort:

> *Dark accurate plunger down the successive knell*
> *Of arch on arch, where ogives burst a red*
> *Reverberance of hail upon the dead*
> *Thunder, like an exploding crucible!*
> *Harshly articulate, musical steel shell*
> *Of angry worship, hurled religiously*
> *Upon your business of humility*
> *Into the iron forestries of hell!*
>
> *Till broken in the shift of quieter*
> *Dense altitudes tangential of your steel,*
> *I am become geometries—and glut*
> *Expansions like a blind astronomer*
> *Dazed, while the worldless heavens bulge and reel*
> *In the cold revery of an idiot.*

The sonnet indicates that the author has faced and defined the possibility of the madness that I have mentioned (a possibility from the consideration of which others as well as himself may have found it impossible to escape) and has arrived at a moral attitude toward it, an attitude which is at once defined and communicated by the poem. This attitude is defined only by the entire poem, not by the logical content alone; it is a matter not only of logical content, but of feeling as well. The feeling is quite specific and unparaphrasable, but one may indicate the nature of it briefly by saying that it is a feeling of dignity and of self-control in the face of a situation of major difficulty, a difficulty which the poet fully apprehends. This feeling is inseparable from what we

4

call poetic form, or unity, for the creation of a form is nothing more nor less than the act of evaluating and shaping (that is, controlling) a given experience. It should be obvious that any attempt to reduce the rational content of such a poem would tend to confuse or even to eliminate the feeling: the poem consists in the relationship between the two.

To reënforce my point, I shall take the liberty of quoting another poem, this one by Mr. Howard Baker, in which something comparable occurs. The title is *Pont Neuf:*

> *Henry the Fourth rides in bronze,*
> *His shoulders curved and pensive, thrust*
> *Enormously into electric*
> *Blazonments of a Christmas trust.*
>
> *Children pass him aghast and pleased,*
> *Reflective of the flickerings*
> *Of jerky bears and clowns. Alone,*
> *Astute to all the bickerings*
>
> *Of age and death rides Henry the Grand.*
> *A lean tug shudders in the Seine;*
> *And Notre Dame is black, a relic*
> *Of the blood of other men.*
>
> *Peace to the other men! And peace*
> *To the mind that has no century,*
> *And sees the savage pull the statue down,*
> *And down the bear and clown.*

The spiritual control in a poem, then, is simply a manifestation of the spiritual control within the poet, and, as I have already indicated, it may have been an important means by which the poet arrived at a realization of spiritual control. This conception must not be confused with the conception of the poem as a safety valve, by which feeling is diverted from action, by which the

5

writer escapes from an attitude by pouring it into his work and leaving it behind him. The conception which I am trying to define is a conception of poetry as a technique of contemplation, of comprehension, a technique which does not eliminate the need of philosophy or of religion, but which, rather, completes and enriches them.

One feels, whether rightly or wrongly, a correlation between the control evinced within a poem and the control within the poet behind it. The laxity of the one ordinarily appears to involve laxity in the other. The rather limp versification of Mr. Eliot and of Mr. MacLeish is inseparable from the spiritual limpness that one feels behind the poems, as the fragmentary, ejaculatory, and over-excited quality of a great many of the poems of Hart Crane is inseparable from the intellectual confusion upon which these particular poems seem to rest (for examples, *The Dance, Cape Hatteras,* and *Atlantis*). Crane possessed great energy, but his faculties functioned clearly only within a limited range of experience (*Repose of Rivers, Voyages II, Faustus and Helen II*). Outside of that range he was either numb (*My Grandmother's Loveletters* and *Harbor Dawn*) or unsure of himself and hence uncertain in his detail (as in *The River,* a very powerful poem in spite of its poor construction and its quantities of bad writing) or both (see *Indiana,* probably one of the worst poems in modern literature). Many of the poems of Mr. Eliot and of Mr. MacLeish could be reduced by paraphrase to about the same thing as my paraphrase of Mr. Tate's sonnet; the difference between them and Mr. Tate in this connection is that, as the form of nearly all of their poems is much looser to start with, the process of paraphrasing would constitute a much slighter act of betrayal. And we must not forget that this quality, form, is not something outside the poet, something "æsthetic," and superimposed upon his moral content; it is essentially a part, in fact it may be the decisive part, of the moral content, even though the poet may be arriving at the final perfection of the condition he is communicating while he communi-

6

cates it and in a large measure as a result of the act and technique of communication. For the communication is first of all with himself: it is, as I have said, the last refinement of contemplation.

I should pause here to remark that many writers have sought to seize the fluidity of experience by breaking down the limits of form, but that in so doing, they defeat their own ends. For, as I have shown, writing, as it approaches the looseness of prose and departs from the strictness of verse, tends to lose the capacity for fluid or highly complex relationships between words; language, in short, reapproaches its original stiffness and generality; and one is forced to recognize the truth of what appears a paradox, that the greatest fluidity of statement is possible where the greatest clarity of form prevails. It is hard to see how the existence of such a work as Mr. Joyce's latest creation [1] can be anything but precarious, in spite of its multitudes of incidental felicities; for it departs from the primary condition of prose—coherent and cumulative logic or narrative—without, since it is, finally, prose, achieving the formal precision of verse. These remarks should not be construed, however, as an argument against free verse, though, with proper qualification, they could be brought to bear in such an argument. The free verse that is really verse—the best, that is, of W. C. Williams, H. D., Miss Moore, Wallace Stevens, and Ezra Pound—is, in its peculiar fashion, the antithesis of free, and the evaluation of this verse is a difficult problem in itself.

Thus we see that the poet, in striving toward an ideal of poetic form at which he has arrived through the study of other poets, is actually striving to perfect a moral attitude toward that range of experience of which he is aware. Such moral attitudes are contagious from poet to poet, and, within the life of a single poet, from poem to poem. The presence of Hardy and Arnold, let us say, in so far as their successful works offer us models and their failures warnings or unfulfilled suggestions, should make it

---

[1] Entitled at this writing (1935) *Work in Progress.*

easier to write good poetry; they should not only aid us, by providing standards of sound feeling, to test the soundness of our own poems, but, since their range of experience is very wide, they should aid us, as we are able to enter and share their experience, to grow into regions that we had not previously mastered or perhaps even discovered. The discipline of imitation is thus valuable if it leads to understanding and assimilation. Too often a minor poet or other reader will recognize in such a master the validity of only that part of the master's experience which corresponds to his own limited range, and will rule out the poetry to which he is consequently numb as sentimental or otherwise imperfect. Inflexibility of critical opinion in such matters is not particularly conducive to growth.

Random experiment may have a related value: one may hit on a form (perhaps the rough idea or draft of a form) which induces some new state or states of mind. I regard as fallacious the notion that form is determined by a precedent attitude or a precedent subject matter, at least invariably: the form (that is, the general idea of a certain type of form) *may* precede, and the attitude, in any case, is never definite till the form is achieved. [1] It does not follow that any attitude resulting from random experiment is intrinsically desirable; undesirable attitudes, like desirable, are contagious and may spread widely; it is here that criticism becomes necessary. A failure, however, to achieve something valuable may offer a valuable suggestion to some one else. The poet who has succeeded once or twice in mastering difficult and central emotions and in recording his mastery for future reference should find it easier to succeed again.

I am not endeavoring in the two foregoing paragraphs to establish poetry as a substitute for philosophy or for religion.

---

[1] As a single example, consider the manner in which the Petrarchan experimenters in England, most of them feeble poets and the best of them given to empty and inflated reasoning, worked out the technique of reasoning elaborately in graceful lyrical verse and bequeathed that technique to the 17th century: the form preceded the matter.

Religion is highly desirable if it is really available to the individual; the study of philosophy is always available and is of incalculable value as a preliminary and as a check to activities as a poet and as a critic (that is, as an intelligent reader). I am, then, merely attempting to define a few of the things which poetry does.

It would perhaps be wise to add another caution: I suffer from no illusion that any man who can write a good poem has a naturally sweet moral temper or that the man who has written three good poems is a candidate for canonization. Literary history is packed with sickening biographies. But it is worth noting that the poetry of such a man, say, as Rochester (who in this is typical of his age) displays a mastery of an extremely narrow range of experience, and that his moral brutality falls almost wholly in those regions (nearly every region save that of worldly manners, if we except some few poems, notably *Upon Nothing, Absent from Thee,* and, possibly, *A Song of a Young Lady to Her Ancient Lover,* in which last there is a curious blending of the erotic with deep moral feeling) with which his poetry fails to deal or with which it deals badly.

This statement requires elucidation. Rochester frequently writes of his debauchery, and sometimes writes well of it, but in the best poems on the subject, in such poems as *The Maim'd Debauchee* and *Upon Drinking in a Bowl,* he writes, as do his contemporaries in the comedy, as a witty and satirical gentleman: the wit inspired by the material is mastered, and other aspects of the material are ignored. In the worst poems on more or less similar material (for examples, the numerous lampoons upon Charles II and upon Nell Gwyn) we have a grossness of feeling comparable to that of his worst actions. All of this, however, detracts not in the least from the quality of Rochester's best poetry, which is remarkably fine; Rochester seldom extends the standards which he recognizes into fields to which they are inapplicable, and hence he is seldom guilty of false evaluation.

9

In reading him, one is aware that he is a sound and beautiful poet, and that there are greater poets. That is all of which one has a right to be aware.[1]

If a poem, in so far as it is good, represents the comprehension on a moral plane of a given experience, it is only fair to add that some experiences offer very slight difficulties and some very great, and that the poem will be the most valuable, which, granted it achieves formal perfection, represents the most difficult victory. In the great tragic poets, such as Racine or Shakespeare, one feels that a victory has been won over life itself, so much is implicated in the subject matter; that feeling is the source of their power over us, whereas a slighter poet will absorb very little of our experience and leave the rest untouched.

This requisite seems to be ignored in a large measure by a good many contemporary poets of more or less mystical tendencies, who avoid the difficult task of mastering the more complex forms of experience by setting up a theoretic escape from them and by then accepting that escape with a good deal of lyrical enthusiasm. Such an escape is offered us, I fear, by Hart Crane, in one of the most extraordinary sections of his volume, *The Bridge*,[2] in the poem called *The Dance*, and such escapes are often employed by Mr. Yeats. In the religious poets of the past, one encounters this vice very seldom; the older religions are fully aware that the heart, to borrow the terms of a poem by Janet Lewis, is untranslatable, whatever may be true of the soul, and that one can escape from the claims of the world only by understanding those claims and by thus accustoming oneself to the thought of eventually putting them by. This necessity is explicitly the subject of one of Sidney's greatest sonnets, *Leave me, O Love, which reachest but to dust,* and of the greatest poem by George Herbert, *Church Monuments;* one can find it

---

[1] *The Collected Poems of John Wilmot, Earl of Rochester,* edited by John Hayward. The Nonesuch Press. 16 Great James St., London, W.C. 1926.

[2] *The Bridge,* by Hart Crane, Horace Liveright: N. Y.: 1930.

10

elsewhere. The attitude is humane, and does not belittle nor evade the magnitude of the task; it is essentially a tragic attitude.

For this reason, the religious fervor of Gerard Hopkins, of John Donne, or of George Herbert should weaken but little the force of most of their poems for the non-believer, just as the deterministic doctrines, whatever their nature and extent, to be found in Hardy, should not weaken for us those poems which do not deal too pugnaciously with the doctrines, and for the same reason. Though a belief in any form of determinism should, if the belief is pushed to its logical ends, eliminate the belief in, and consequently the functioning of, whatever it is that we call the will, yet there is no trace of any kind of disintegration in Hardy's poetic style, in his sense of form, which we have seen to be, so far as writing is concerned, identical with the will or the ability to control and shape one's experience. The tragic necessity of putting by the claims of the world without the abandonment of self-control, without loss of the ability to go on living, for the present, intelligently and well, is just as definitely the subject of Hardy's poetry as of Herbert's. We have in both poets a common moral territory which is far greater than are the theological regions which they do not share; for, on the one hand, the fundamental concepts of morality are common to intelligent men regardless of theological orientation, except in so far as morality may be simply denied or ignored, and, on the other hand, the Absolute is in its nature inscrutable and offers little material for speculation, except in so far as it is a stimulus to moral speculation. It would be difficult, I think, to find a devotional poem of which most of the implications were not moral and universal. So with Hardy: his determinism was mythic and animistic and tended to dramatize the human struggle, whereas a genuinely rational and coherent determinism would have eliminated the human struggle. He was thrown back upon traditional literary and folk wisdom in working out moral situations, and for these situations his mythology provided a

11

new setting, sometimes magnificent, sometimes melodramatic, but, thanks to its rational incompleteness, not really destructive of a working morality. Like many another man who has been unable to think clearly, he was saved by the inability to think coherently: had he been coherent, he would probably have been about as interesting as Godwin; as it is, his professed beliefs and his working beliefs have only a little in common, and the former damage his work only in a fragmentary way, as when satires of circumstance are dragged into a novel or isolated in a poem to prove a point (and they can prove nothing, of course) and usually to the detriment of coherent feeling and understanding.

Crane's attitude, on the other hand, often suggests a kind of theoretic rejection of all human endeavor in favor of some vaguely apprehended but ecstatically asserted existence of a superior sort. As the exact nature of the superior experience is uncertain, it forms a rather uncertain and infertile source of material for exact poetry; one can write poetry about it only by utilizing in some way more or less metaphorical the realm of experience from which one is trying to escape; but as one *is* endeavoring to escape from this realm, not to master it and understand it, one's feelings about it are certain to be confused, and one's imagery drawn from it is bound to be largely formulary and devoid of meaning. That is, in so far as one endeavors to deal with the Absolute, not as a means of ordering one's moral perception but as the subject itself of perception, one will tend to say nothing, despite the multiplication of words. In *The Dance* there seems to be an effort to apply to each of two mutually exclusive fields the terms of the other. This is a vice of which Rochester was not guilty.

Crane's best work, such as *Repose of Rivers* and *Voyages II,* is not confused, but one feels that the experience is curiously limited and uncomplicated: it is between the author, isolated from most human complications, and Eternity. Crane becomes in

12

such poems a universal symbol of the human mind in a particular situation, a fact which is the source of his power, but of the human mind in very nearly the simplest form of that situation, a fact which is the source of his limitation.

Objective proof of this assertion cannot be found in the poems, any more than proof of the opposite quality can be found in Hardy; it is in each poet a matter of feeling invading the poetry mainly by way of the non-paraphrasable content: one feels the fragility of Crane's finest work, just as one feels the richness of Hardy's. Hardy is able to utilize, for example, great ranges of literary, historical, and other connotations in words and cadences; one feels behind each word the history of the word and the generations of men who embodied that history; Hardy gets somehow at the wealth of the race. It should be observed again how the moral discipline is involved in the literary discipline, how it becomes, at times, almost a matter of living philology. From the greater part of this wealth Crane appears to be isolated and content to remain isolated. His isolation, like Hardy's immersion, was in part social and unavoidable, but a clearer mind and a more fixed intention might have overcome much of the handicap.

I should like to forestall one possible objection to the theory of poetry which I am trying to elucidate. Poetry, as a moral discipline, should not be regarded as one more means of escape. That is, moral responsibility should not be transferred from action to paper in the face of a particular situation. Poetry, if pursued either by the poet or by the reader, in the manner which I have suggested, should offer a means of enriching one's awareness of human experience and of so rendering greater the possibility of intelligence in the course of future action; and it should offer likewise a means of inducing certain more or less constant habits of feeling, which should render greater the possibility of one's acting, in a future situation, in accordance with the findings of one's improved intelligence. It should, in other words, increase the intelligence and strengthen the moral

13

temper; these effects should naturally be carried over into action, if, through constant discipline, they are made permanent acquisitions. If the poetic discipline is to have steadiness and direction, it requires an antecedent discipline of ethical thinking and of at least some ethical feeling, which may be in whole or in part the gift of religion or of a social tradition, or which may be largely the result of individual acquisition by way of study. The poetic discipline includes the antecedent discipline and more: it is the richest and most perfect technique of contemplation.

This view of poetry in its general outline is not original, but is a restatement of ideas that have been current in English criticism since the time of Sidney, that have appeared again in most of the famous apologists for poetry since Sidney, especially in Arnold and in Newman. In summarizing these ideas, I have merely endeavored to illuminate a few of the more obscure relationships and to dispose of them in such a way as to prepare the reader for various analyses of poetic method which I intend, in other essays, to undertake. Poetic morality and poetic feeling are inseparable; feeling and technique, or structure, are inseparable. Technique has laws which govern poetic (and perhaps more general) morality more widely than is commonly recognized. It is my intention to examine them.

THE EXPERIMENTAL SCHOOL IN AMERICAN POETRY

An Analytical Survey of Its Structural Methods,
Exclusive of Meter

DURING the second and third decades of the twentieth century, the chief poetic talent of the United States took certain new directions, directions that appear to me in the main regrettable. The writers between Robinson and Frost, on the one hand, and Allen Tate and Howard Baker on the other, who remained relatively traditional in manner were with few exceptions minor or negligible; the more interesting writers, as I shall endeavor to show in these pages, were misguided, and in discussing them I shall have little to say of their talents, their ineliminable virtues, but shall rather take these for granted.

In order that I may evaluate the new structural methods, I shall have first to describe at least briefly the old. Inasmuch as a wider range of construction is possible in the short poem than in any of the longer literary forms, I shall deal with principles that are fundamental to all literary composition, and shall here and there have recourse to illustrations drawn from the novel or perhaps from the drama. The virtues of the traditional modes of construction will be indicated chiefly in connection with my discussion of the defects of the recent experimental modes.

TYPE I: THE METHOD OF REPETITION

Kenneth Burke has named and described this method without evaluating it.[1] It is the simplest and most primitive method possible, and is still in common use; if limited to a short lyrical

---

[1] In *Counterstatement* (Harcourt, Brace and Co.: 1932).

15

form, it may still be highly effective. It consists in a restatement in successive stanzas of a single theme, the terms, or images, being altered in each restatement. Two of the finest poems in the form are Nashe's poem on the plague (*Adieu! Farewell earth's bliss*) and Raleigh's poem entitled *The Lie.* In such a poem there is no rational necessity for any order of sequence, the order being determined wholly by the author's feeling about the graduation of importance or intensity. Nevertheless, such a poem rests on a formulable logic, however simple; that is, the theme can be paraphrased in general terms. Such a paraphrase, of course, is not the equivalent of a poem: a poem is more than its paraphrasable content. But, as we shall eventually see, many poems cannot be paraphrased and are therefore defective.

The method of repetition is essentially the same today as it has always been, if we confine our attention to the short poem. Of recent years, however, there has been a tendency to extend it into longer forms, with unfortunate results. Such extension is the chief method of Whitman, and results in a form both lax and diffuse. Such extension occurs even in many modern attempts at narrative, both in prose and in verse. To illustrate what I say, I shall venture to summarize the structural defects of the narrative poetry of Robinson Jeffers:

Mr. Jeffers is theologically some kind of monist. He envisages, as did Wordsworth, nature as Deity; but his Nature is the Nature of the text-book in physics and not that of the rambling botanist—Mr. Jeffers seems to have taken the terminology of modern physics more literally than it is meant by its creators. Nature, or God, is thus a kind of self-sufficient mechanism, of which man is a product, but from which man is cut off by his humanity (just what gave rise to this humanity, which is absolutely severed from all communication with God, is left for others to decide): as there is no mode of communication with God or from God, God is praised adequately only by the screaming demons that make up the atom. Man, if he accepts

16

this dilemma as necessary, can choose between two modes of action: he may renounce God and rely upon his humanity, or he may renounce his humanity and rely upon God.

In the narratives preceding *Cawdor* [1] and in most of the lyrics, Mr. Jeffers preaches the second choice. In *Cawdor* and in *Thurso's Landing,* [2] he has attempted a compromise: that is, while the tragic characters recognize that the second choice would be the more reasonable, they make the first in a kind of half-hearted stubbornness. They insist on living, but without knowing why, and without any good to which to look forward save the final extinction in God, when it comes in God's time. Their stubbornness is meaningless.

Life as such is incest, an insidious and destructive evil. So much, says Mr. Jeffers by implication, for Greek and Christian ethics. Now the mysticism of such a man as San Juan de la Cruz offers at least the semblance of a spiritual, a human, discipline as a preliminary to union with Divinity; but for Mr. Jeffers a simple and mechanical device lies always ready; namely, suicide, a device to which he has, I believe, never resorted.

In refusing to take this step, however, Mr. Jeffers illustrates one of a very interesting series of romantic compromises. The romantic of the ecstatically pantheistic type denies life yet goes on living; [3] nearly all romantics decry the intellect and philosophy, yet they offer justifications, necessarily incoherent but none the less rational in intention, of their attitude; they are prone to belittle literary technique, yet they write, and too often with small efficiency; they preach, in the main, the doctrine of moral equivalence, yet their every action, whether private or literary, since it rests on a choice, is a denial of the doctrine. Not

---

[1] *Cawdor and Other Poems,* by Robinson Jeffers. Horace Liveright, New York, 1928.

[2] *Thurso's Landing,* same. Liveright Inc., New York, 1932.

[3] Hart Crane, unlike Mr. Jeffers, demonstrated the seriousness of his conviction, but the demonstration did nothing to clarify his concepts.

all romantics are guilty of all these forms of confusion, but the romantic who is guilty of all is more consistent than is he who is guilty only of some, for all inhere in each from a rational standpoint. And Mr. Jeffers, having decried human life, and having denied the worth of the rules of the game, endeavors to write narrative and dramatic poems, poems, in other words, dealing with people who are playing the game. Jesus, the hero of *Dear Judas*,[1] speaking apparently for Mr. Jeffers, says that the secret reason for the doctrine of forgiveness is that all men are driven to act as they do, by the mechanism-God, that they are entirely helpless; yet he adds in the next breath that this secret must be guarded, for if it were given out, men would run amuck—they would begin acting differently.[2]

The Women at Point Sur[3] is a perfect laboratory of Mr. Jeffers' philosophy and a perfect example of his narrative method. Barclay, an insane divine, preaches Mr. Jeffers' religion, and his disciples, acting upon it, become emotional mechanisms, lewd and twitching conglomerations of plexuses, their humanity annuled. Human experience in these circumstances, having necessarily and according to the doctrine, no meaning, there can be no necessary sequence of events: every act is equivalent to every other; every act is devoid of consequence and occurs in a perfect vacuum; most of the incidents could be shuffled about into different sequences without violating anything save Mr. Jeffers' sense of their relative intensity.

Since the poem is his, of course, this sense may appear a legitimate criterion; the point is, that this is not a narrative nor a dramatic but is a lyrical criterion. A successful lyrical poem of one hundred and seventy-five pages is unlikely, for the essence of

---

[1] *Dear Judas* (Horace Liveright: 1929).

[2] This dilemma is not new in American literature. In the eighteenth century, Jonathan Edwards accomplished a revival in the Puritan Church, that is, induced large numbers of sinners to repent and enter the church, by preaching the doctrine of election and the inability to repent.

[3] *The Women at Point Sur* (Boni and Liveright: 1927).

18

lyrical expression is concentration; but it is at least hypothetically possible. The difficulty here is that the lyric achieves its effect by the generalization of experience (that is, the motivation of the lyric is stated or implied in a summary form, and is ordinarily not given in detailed narrative) and by the concentration of expression; lyrical poetry tends to be expository. Narrative can survive fairly well without distinction of style, provided the narrative logic is complete and compelling, as in the works of Balzac, though this occurs most often in prose. Now Mr. Jeffers, as I have pointed out, has abandoned narrative logic with the theory of ethics, and he has never, in addition, achieved a distinguished style: his writing, line by line, is pretentious trash. There are a few good phrases, but they are very few, and none is first-rate.

Mr. Jeffers has no method of sustaining his lyric, then, other than the employment of an accidental (that is, a non-narrative and repetitious) series of anecdotes (that is, of details that are lyrically impure, details clogged with too much information to be able to function properly as lyrical details); his philosophical doctrine and his artistic dilemma alike decree that these shall be at an hysterical pitch of feeling. By this method, Mr. Jeffers continually *lays claim* to extreme feeling, which has no support whether of structure or of detail and which is therefore simply unmastered and self-inflicted hysteria.

Cawdor contains a plot which in its rough outlines might be sound, and *Cawdor* likewise contains his best poetry: the lines describing the seals at dawn, especially, are very good. But the plot is blurred for lack of style and for lack of moral intelligence on the part of the author. As in *Thurso's Landing*, of which the writing is much worse, the protagonists desire to live as the result of a perfectly unreasoning and meaningless stubbornness, and their actions are correspondingly obscure. Mr. Jeffers will not even admit the comprehensible motive of cowardice. In

19

The Tower beyond Tragedy,[1] Mr. Jeffers takes one of the very best of ready-made plots, the Orestes-Clytemnestra situation, the peculiar strength of which lies in the fact that Orestes is forced to choose between two crimes, the murder of his mother and the failure to avenge his father. But at the very last moment, in Mr. Jeffers' version, Orestes is converted to Mr. Jeffers' religion and goes off explaining to Electra (who has just tried to seduce him) that though men may think he is fleeing from the furies, he is really doing no more than drift up to the mountains to meditate on the stars. And the preceding action is, of course, rendered meaningless.

Dear Judas is a kind of dilution of *The Women at Point Sur*, with Jesus as Barclay, and with a less detailed background. *The Loving Shepherdess*[2] deals with a girl who knows herself doomed to die at a certain time in child-birth, and who wanders over the countryside caring for a small and diminishing flock of sheep in an anguish of devotion. The events here also are anecdotal and reversible, and the feeling is lyrical or nothing. The heroine is turned cruelly from door to door, and the sheep fall one by one before the reader's eyes, the sheep and the doors constituting the matter of the narrative; until finally the girl dies in a ditch in an impossible effort to give birth to her child.

TYPE II: THE LOGICAL METHOD

By the logical method of composition, I mean simply explicitly rational progression from one detail to another: the poem has a clearly evident expository structure. Marvell's poem *To His Coy Mistress,* as Mr. T. S. Eliot has said, has something of the structure of a syllogism, if the relationships only of the three paragraphs to each other be considered:[3] within each para-

---

[1] In the volume called *The Women at Point Sur*, previously mentioned.
[2] In the volume entitled *Dear Judas.*
[3] *Selected Essays,* by T. S. Eliot. Harcourt, Brace and Co., New York: 1932.

graph the structure is repetitive. The logical method is a late and sophisticated procedure that in Europe is most widespread in the sixteenth and seventeenth centuries, though it appears earlier and continues later. It was exploited, mastered, and frequently debauched by the English Metaphysical School, for example, though it was not invariably employed by them.

Sometimes in the Metaphysical poets, frequently in the dramatists contemporary with them, and far too often in the poetry of the twentieth century, the logical structure becomes a shell empty of logic but exploiting certain elusive types of feeling. The forms of pseudo-logic I shall reserve for treatment under another heading.

By stretching our category a trifle we may include under this heading poems *implicitly* rational, provided the implications of rationality are at all points clear. William Carlos Williams' poem, *On the Road to the Contagious Hospital,* may serve as an example.[1] On the other hand, Rimbaud's *Larme,* a poem which, like that of Dr. Williams, describes a landscape, is unformulable: it is an example of what Kenneth Burke has called qualitative progression, a type of procedure that I shall consider later. The poem by Williams, though its subject is simple, is a poem of directed meditation; the poem by Rimbaud is one of non-rational and hallucinatory terror.

TYPE III: NARRATIVE

Narrative achieves coherence largely through a feeling that the events of a sequence are necessary parts of a causative chain, or plausible interferences with a natural causative chain. In this it is similar to logic. The hero, being what he is and in a given situation, seems to act naturally or unnaturally; if his

---

[1] *Spring and All,* by William Carlos Williams. Contact Editions, Paris. The poem is quoted in full in the essay on *Poetic Convention,* in this book.

21

action seems natural, and is in addition reasonably interesting and, from an ethical point of view, important, the narrative is in the main successful. To this extent, Mr. Kenneth Burke is wrong, I believe, in censuring nineteenth century fiction for its concern with what he calls the psychology of the hero as opposed to the concern with the psychology of the audience:[1] by the former, he means the plausibility of the portrait; by the latter the concern with those rhetorical devices which please and surprise the reader, devices, for example, of the type of which Fielding was a consummate master. Mr. Burke overlooks the facts that rhetoric cannot exist without a subject matter, and that the subject matter of fiction is narration, that, in short, the author's most important instrument for controlling the attitude of the audience is precisely the psychology of the hero. Mr. Burke is right, however, in that there are other, less important but necessary means of controlling the attitude of the audience, and that most of the standard fiction of the nineteenth century, sometimes for neglecting them, sometimes for utilizing them badly, suffers considerably.

Mr. Burke, in his own compositions, with a precocious security that is discouraging, reverses the Victorian formula: in his novel, *Towards a Better Life*,[2] he concentrates on the sentence, or occasionally on the paragraph, that is, on the incidental. He has attained what appears to be his chief end: he has made himself quotable. His book contains some good aphorisms and many bad; it contains some excellent interludes, such as the fable of the scholar with the face like a vegetable, or the paragraph on Voltaire. Any of these felicities may be removed from their context with perfect impunity, for there really is no context: *Towards a Better Life*, as a whole, is duller than Thackeray. On the other hand, such writers as Jane Austen and Edith

---

[1] In the volume called *Counterstatement,* already mentioned.

[2] *Towards a Better Life,* by Kenneth Burke. Harcourt, Brace and Co.: New York: 1932.

Wharton are likely to be wittier than Mr. Burke; but their wit, like that of Molière, is not often separable from their context, since it is primarily a context that they are creating.

Short sketches in prose often deal with the revelation of a situation instead of with the development of one. The result is static, but if the prose is skillful and does not run to excessive length, it may be successful: Cunninghame Graham's *At Dalmary* [1] is a fine example. Other things being equal, however (which, of course, they never are), action should lend power. In a short narrative poem it matters little whether the situation be revealed or developed: the force of the poetic language can raise the statement to great impressiveness either way; in fact, the process of revelation itself may take on in a short poem a quality profoundly dramatic. [2] The famous English Ballad, *Edward,* Mr. E. A. Robinson's *Luke Havergal,* [3] *Her Going* [4] by Agnes Lee, are all examples of revelation at a high level of excellence. Mr. Robinson's *Eros Turannos* [3] is a fine example of development within a short form.

The coherence of character may be demonstrated, as in the novels of Henry James, in a closed, or dramatic plot, in which personage acts upon personage, and in which accident and mechanical change play little part; or the personage may prove himself coherent in a struggle with pure accident, as in Defoe, who pits Moll Flanders against the wilderness of London, or as in Melville, who pits Ahab against the complex wilderness of the sea, of brute nature, and of moral evil; or there may be, as in Mrs. Wharton, a merging of the two extremes: in Mrs. Wharton, the impersonal adversary is usually represented by a human

---

[1] *Hope,* by Cunninghame Graham. Duckeworth, London.

[2] It is curious that this procedure if employed in a long form, such as the novel or the play, tends to degenerate into bald melodrama; it is the essential, for example, of detective fiction. On the other hand, it is in a large part the form of *The Ambassadors,* the revelation in this, however, motivating further development.

[3] *Collected Poems,* by E. A. Robinson: MacMillan.

[4] *Faces and Open Doors,* by Agnes Lee. R. F. Seymour, Chicago, 1932.

being such as Undine Spragg or the elder Raycie, who is morally or intellectually undeveloped, so that the protagonist is unable to cope with him in human terms. The novel is not the drama, and to demand of it dramatic plot appears to me unreasonable. The form permits the treatment of a great deal of material impossible in the drama, and the material, since it is important in human life, ought to be treated. It is certain, however, that narrative requires coherence of character, and coherence necessitates change. Fielding is dull in bulk because his characters do not develop and because his incidents are without meaning except as anecdotal excuses for the exercise of style. Defoe's rhetoric is less agile, but his conception is more solid.

In addition to having greater range, the novel of accident may have advantages over the dramatic novel which are perhaps too seldom considered. The author is less likely to be restricted to the exact contents of the minds of his characters, and so he may have greater opportunity to exhibit, directly or indirectly, his own attitudes, which, in most cases, may be more complex than the attitudes of his characters. Fielding, for example, would have been seriously embarrassed to treat Tom Jones from the point of view of Tom Jones. Melville accomplishes even more with his personal freedom than does Fielding. The superstition that the author should write wholly from within the minds of his characters appears to have grown up largely as a reaction to the degeneration of Fieldingese among the Victorians, notably Thackeray and Dickens, and perhaps Meredith, and perhaps in part as a result of the achievements in the newer mode by Flaubert and by Henry James. Flaubert is misleading, however, in that the perfection and subtlety of his style introduces an important element from without the consciousness of the character in a manner that may be overlooked; and James is misleading not only in this respect but because his characters are usually almost as highly developed as the author himself, so that the two are frequently all but indistinguishable. The superstition is reduced to absurdity in some of Mr. Hemingway's short stories about prize-fighters and bull-fighters, whose views of their own experience are about as valuable as the views of the Sunbonnet Babies or of Little Black Sambo.

Theoretically, that fictional convention should be most desirable which should allow the author to deal with a character from a position formally outside the mind of the character, and which should allow him to analyze, summarize, and arrange material, as author, and without regard to the way in which the character might be supposed to have perceived the material originally. This procedure should permit the greatest possibility of rhetorical range; should permit the direct play of the intelligence of the author, over and above the intelligence and limitations of the character; it should permit the greatest possible attention to what Mr. Kenneth Burke has called the psychology of the audience in so far as it is separable from what he calls the psychology of the hero: Mr. Burke, in fact, in his own novel, *Towards a Better Life,* employs a modified stream-of-consciousness convention, thus limiting the rhetorical range very narrowly, and confining himself to a very narrow aspect of the psychology of the hero, so far as the construction of his work as a whole is concerned, and in a large measure as regards all relationships beyond those within the individual sentence. The convention which I should recommend is that of the first-rate biography or history (Johnson's *Lives,* for example, or Hume, or Macaulay) instead of the various post-Joycean conventions now prevalent. Exposition may be made an art; so may historical summary; in fact, the greatest prose in existence is that of the greatest expository writers. The novel should not forego these sources of strength. If it be argued that the first aim of the novelist is to reach a public from whom the great expositors are isolated by their very virtues, then the novelist is in exactly that measure unworthy of serious discussion. My recommendation is not made wholly in the absence of examples, however: allowances made for

25

individual limitations of scope and defects of procedure, Jane Austen, Melville, Hawthorne, Henry James, Fielding, and Defoe may be called to serve; Edith Wharton at her best, in such performances as *Bunner Sisters* and *False Dawn*, as *The Valley of Decision* and *The Age of Innocence*, is nearly the perfect example.

TYPE IV: PSEUDO-REFERENCE

Every line or passage of good poetry, every good poetic phrase, communicates a certain quality of feeling as well as a certain paraphrasable content. It would be possible to write a poem unimpeachable as to rational sequence, yet wholly inconsecutive in feeling or even devoid of feeling. Meredith and Browning often display both defects. Chapman's *Hero and Leander* is a rational continuation of Marlowe's beginning, but the break in feeling is notorious.

Suppose that we imagine the reversal of this formula, retaining in our language coherence of feeling, but as far as possible reducing rational coherence. The reduction may be accomplished in either of two ways: (1) we may retain the syntactic forms and much of the vocabulary of rational coherence, thus aiming to exploit the feeling of rational coherence in its absence or at least in excess of its presence; or (2) we may abandon all pretence of rational coherence. The first of these methods I have called *pseudo-reference* and shall treat in this section. The second I shall reserve for the next section.

Pseudo-reference takes a good many forms. I shall list as many forms as I have observed. My list will probably not be complete, but it will be nearly enough complete to illustrate the principle and to provide a basis of further observation.

1. *Grammatical coherence in excess of, or in the absence of, rational coherence.* This may mean no more than a slight excess of grammatical machinery, a minor redundancy. Thus Miss Moore, in *Black Earth*:

26

> *I do these*
> *things which I do, which please*
> *no one but myself.*[1]

The words which I have set in Roman are redundant. Again, in *Reinforcements,*[1] Miss Moore writes:

> *the future of time is determined by*
> *the power of volition*

when she means:

> *volition determines the future.*

Miss Moore is usually ironic when writing thus, but not always; and I confess that it appears to me a somewhat facile and diffuse kind of irony, for the instrument of irony (the poetry) is weakened in the interests of irony. It is an example of what I shall have repeated occasion to refer to as the fallacy of expressive, or imitative, form; the procedure in which the form succumbs to the raw material of the poem. It is as if Dryden had descended to imitating Shadwell's style in his efforts to turn it to ridicule.

Closely related to this procedure, but much more audacious, is the maintenance of grammatical coherence when there is no coherence of thought or very little. Hart Crane, for example, has placed at the beginning of his poem, *For the Marriage of Faustus and Helen,*[2] the following quotation from Ben Jonson's play, *The Alchemist*:

> *And so we may arrive by Talmud skill*
> *And profane Greek to raise the building up*
> *Of Helen's house against the Ismaelite,*
> *King of Thogarma, and his habergeons*
> *Brimstony, blue and fiery; and the force*

---

[1] *Observations*, by Marianne Moore. The Dial Press: N. Y. 1924.
[2] *White Buildings*, by Hart Crane. Boni and Liveright: 1926.

Of King Abaddon, and the beast of Cittim;
Which Rabbi David Kimchi, Onkelos,
And Aben Ezra do interpret Rome.[1]

This is one of the numerous passages in the play, in which the characters speak nonsense purporting to contain deep alchemical secrets or to express a feignedly distraught state of mind: this particular passage serves both functions at once. The nonsense is necessary to Jonson's plot; the reader recognizes the necessity and can make no objection, so that he is forced to accept with unalloyed pleasure whatever elusive but apparently real poetic implications there may be in such a passage, since he receives these implications absolutely gratis. The technique of expressive form, to which I have alluded, is here forced upon Jonson in a measure by the dramatic medium, for the characters must be represented in their own persons; this may or may not indicate a defect in the medium itself, as compared to other methods of satire, but at any rate there is no misuse of the medium. Jonson appears, then, to have been wholly aware of this procedure, which is usually regarded as a Mallarmean or Rimbaldian innovation, and Crane appears to have found at least one of his chief models for this kind of writing in Jonson. Jonson differs from Crane in that he does not employ the method when writing in his own name, but merely employs it to characterize his cozeners.

The two sections in blank verse of *Faustus and Helen* resemble Jonson's nonsense very closely. For example:

> *The mind is brushed by sparrow wings;*
> *Numbers, rebuffed by asphalt, crowd*
> *The margins of the day, accent the curbs,*
> *Conveying divers dawns on every corner*

---

[1] Act IV: 3.

> *To druggist, barber, and tobacconist,*
> *Until the graduate opacities of evening*
> *Take them away as suddenly to somewhere*
> *Virginal, perhaps, less fragmentary, cool.*

This is perfectly grammatical, and if not examined too carefully may appear more or less comprehensible. But the activities of the numbers, if the entire sentence is surveyed, appear wholly obscure. If one suppose *numbers* to be a synonym for *numbers of persons,* for *crowds,* one or two points are cleared up, but no more. If one suppose the numbers to be the mathematical abstractions of modern life, structural, temporal, financial, and others similar, there is greater clarity; but the first five lines are so precious and indirect as to be somewhat obscure, and the last three lines are perfectly obscure.

There is a pleasanter example of the same kind of writing in a shorter poem by Crane, and from the same volume, the poem called *Sunday Morning Apples:*

> *A boy runs with a dog before the sun, straddling*
> *Spontaneities that form their independent orbits,*
> *Their own perennials of light*
> *In the valley where you live*
>
> > *(called Brandywine.)*

The second line, taken in conjunction with the first, conveys the action of the boy, but it does so indirectly and by suggestion. What it says, if we consider rational content alone, is really indecipherable. One can, of course, make a rational paraphrase, but one can do it, not by seeking the rational content of the lines, but by seeking suggestions as to the boy's behavior, and by then making a rational statement regarding it. The line has a certain loveliness and conveys what it sets out to convey: the objection which I should make to it is that it goes through certain motions that are only half effective. A greater poet would have made the

29

rational formula count rationally, at the same time that he was utilizing suggestion; he would thus have achieved a more concentrated poetry.

2. *Transference of Values from one field of experience to another and unrelated field.* I shall illustrate this procedure with passages from Crane's poem, *The Dance.*[1] The poem opens with the description of a journey first by canoe up the Hudson, then on foot into the mountains. As the protagonist, or narrator, proceeds on his way, he appears to proceed likewise into the past, until he arrives at the scene of an Indian dance, at which a chieftain, Maquokeeta, is being burned at the stake. The poem from this point on deals with the death and apotheosis of Maquokeeta, the apotheosis taking the form of a union with Pocahontas, who has been introduced in this poem and in the poem preceding, *The River,* as a kind of mythic deity representing the American soil. The following passage is the climax and the most striking moment in the poem:

> *O, like the lizard in the furious noon,*
> *That drops his legs and colors in the sun,*
> *—And laughs, pure serpent, Time itself, and moon*
> *Of his own fate, I saw thy change begun!*
>
> *And saw thee dive to kiss that destiny*
> *Like one white meteor, sacrosanct and blent*
> *At last with all that's consummate and free*
> *There where the first and last gods keep thy tent.*

The remainder of the poem develops the same theme and the same mood. The following phrases are typical:

> *Thy freedom is her largesse, Prince . . .*
> *And are her perfect brows to thine? . . .*

---

[1] From *The Bridge,* by Hart Crane. Horace Liveright, N. Y.: 1930.

30

The difficulty resides in the meaning of the union. It may be regarded in either of two ways: as the simple annihilation and dissolution in the soil of Maquokeeta, or as the entrance into another and superior mode of life. There is no possible compromise.

If we select the former alternative, the language of mystical and physical union has no relationship to the event: it is language carried over, with all or a good deal of its connotation, from two entirely different realms of experience. The passage is thus parasitic for its effect upon feelings unrelated to its theme. The words *consummate and free,* for example, carry the connotations common to them, but their rational meaning in this context is *terminated and dissipated. Sacrosanct,* similarly, while carrying certain feelings from its religious past, would mean *devoid of human meaning,* or, more concisely, *devoid of meaning.* Similarly, *perfect,* in the last line quoted, carries feelings from love poetry, but it would actually signify *meaningless.* In other words, extinction is beatitude. But this is nonsense: extinction is extinction. If there is a state of beatitude, it is a state; that is, it is not extinction.

If we accept the second alternative and assume that some really mystical experience is implied, there is nothing in the poem or elsewhere in Crane's work to give us a clue to the nature of the experience. The only possible conclusion is that he was confused as to his own feelings and did not bother to find out what he was really talking about. That odd bits of this obscurity can be glossed I am fully aware; but it cannot be cleaned up to an extent even moderately satisfactory. There is a wide margin of obscurity and of meaningless excitement, despite a certain splendor of language which may at times move one to forget, or to try to forget, what the poem lacks.

Further, there seems actually little doubt that Crane did confuse in some way the ideas of extinction and of beatitude, and that he was an enthusiastic pantheistical mystic. The mere fact

31

that beatitude is represented in this poem by the union with Pocahontas, who stands for the soil of America, is evidence in itself; and further evidence may be found in *The River* and in some of the shorter poems. But one does not create a religion and a conception of immortality simply by naming the soil Pocahontas and by then writing love poetry to the Indian girl who bore that name. Crane repeatedly refers to an idea which he cannot define and which probably never had even potential existence.

A similar difficulty occurs in *Atlantis,* the final section of *The Bridge,* the sequence of which *The Dance* and *The River* are central parts. The Brooklyn Bridge is seen in a kind of vision or hallucination as the new Atlantis, the future America. The language is ecstatic; at certain moments and in certain ways it comes near to being the most brilliant language in Crane's work:

> *Like hails, farewells—up planet-sequined heights*
> *Some trillion whispering hammers glimmer Tyre:*
> *Serenely, sharply up the long anvil cry*
> *Of inchling æons silence rivets Troy . . .*

But the only poetic embodiment of the future, the only source of the ecstacy, is a quantitative vision of bigger cities with higher buildings. One can read a certain amount of allegory into this, but in so far as one makes the allegory definite or comprehensible, one will depart from the text; the enthusiasm again is obscure.

3. *Reference to a non-existent plot.* This is most easily illustrated by selections from T. S. Eliot. I quote from *Gerontion:* [1]

> *To be eaten, to be divided, to be drunk*
> *Among whispers; by Mr. Silvero*
> *With caressing hands, at Limoges*
> *Who walked all night in the next room;*

---

[1] *Poems 1909-1925,* by T. S. Eliot.

By Hakagawa, bowing among the Titians;
By Madame de Tornquist, in the dark room
Shifting the candles; Fräulein von Kulp
Who turned in the hall, one hand on the door.

Each one of these persons is denoted in the performance of an act, and each act, save possibly that of Hakagawa, implies an anterior situation, is a link in a chain of action; even that of Hakagawa implies an anterior and unexplained personality. Yet we have no hint of the nature of the history implied. A feeling is claimed by the poet, the motivation, or meaning, of which is with-held, and of which in all likelihood he has no clearer notion than his readers can have. I do not wish to seem to insist that Mr. Eliot should have recounted the past histories in order to perfect this particular poem. Given the convention, the modus operandi, the obscurity is inevitable, and compared to the obscurity which we have just seen in Crane, it is relatively innocent. But obscurity it is: discreetly modulated diffuseness. A more direct and economical convention seems to me preferable.

Mr. Eliot does much the same thing, but less skillfully, else-where. The following passage is from *Burbank with a Baedecker; Bleistein with a Cigar:* [1]

Burbank crossed a little bridge,
Descending at a small hotel;
Princess Volupine arrived,
They were together, and he fell.

What is the significance of the facts in the first two lines? They have no real value as perception: the notation is too perfunctory. They must have some value as information, as such details might have value, for example, in a detective story, if they are to have any value at all. Yet they have no bearing on what follows; in fact, most of what follows is obscure in exactly the same way. They are not even necessary to what occurs in the next two lines,

---

[1] *Poems 1909-1925*, by T. S. Eliot.

for Princess Volupine might just as well have encountered him anywhere else and after any other transit.

4. *Explicit Reference to a non-existent symbolic value.* The following lines are taken from a poem entitled *Museum*,[1] by Mr. Alan Porter:

> *The day was empty. Very pale with dust,*
> *A chalk road set its finger at the moors.*
> *The drab, damp air so blanketed the town*
> *Never an oak swung leather leaf. The chimneys*
> *Pushed up their pillars at the loose-hung sky;*
> *And through the haze, along the ragstone houses,*
> *Red lichens dulled to a rotten-apple brown.*
>
> .   .   .   .   .
>
> *Suddenly turning a byeway corner, a cripple,*
> *Bloodless with age, lumbered along the road.*
> *The motes of dust whirled at his iron-shod crutches*
> *And quickly settled. A dog whined. The old*
> *Cripple looked round, and, seeing no man, gave*
> *A quick, small piping chuckle, swung a pace,*
> *And stopped to look about and laugh again.*
> *"That," said a girl in a flat voice, "is God."*
> *Her mother made no answer; she remembered,*
> *"I knew an old lame beggar who went mad."*
> *He lumbered along the road and turned a corner.*
> *His tapping faded and the day was death.*

This poem is ably written and has an unusually fine texture; in fact, it is the texture of the entire work which provides the effective setting for the factitious comment on the beggar, and the comment is introduced with great skill. The landscape is intense and mysterious, as if with meaning withheld. In such a setting,

---

[1] *Signature of Pain,* by Alan Porter. The John Day Company: New York: 1931.

34

the likening of the beggar to God appears, for an instant, portentous, but only for an instant, for there is no discernible basis for the likening. The beggar is treated as if he were symbolic of something, whereas he is really symbolic of nothing that one can discover. The introduction of the beggar appears to be a very skillful piece of sleight-of-hand; yet it is not an incidental detail of the description, but is rather the climax of the description, the theme of the poem. We have, in other words, a rather fine poem about nothing.

5. *Implicit Reference to a non-existent symbolic value.* It may be difficult at times to distinguish this type of pseudo-reference from the last or from the type which I have designated under the heading of transferred value. I shall merely endeavor to select examples as obvious as possible.

There is, in the first place, such a thing as implicit reference to a genuine symbolic value. The second sonnet in Heredia's *Trophées,* the sonnet entitled *Némée,* describes the slaying of the Nemean lion by Hercules. Hercules is the typical hero; the slaying of the lion is the heroic task; the fleeing peasant is the common mortal for whom the task is performed. It is nakedly and obviously allegorical, yet there is no statement within the poem of the allegorical intention: it is our familiarity with the myth and with other similar myths which makes us recognize the poem as allegory. Similarly, there is no statement of allegorical intention within Blake's poem, *The Tiger:* the recognition of the intention is due to Blake's having been fairly explicit in other works.

Further, it is possible to describe an item with no past history in such a way that it will have a significance fairly general. This is the procedure of a handful of the best poems of the Imagist movement; for example, of Dr. Williams' poem, *On the road to the contagious hospital.* Thus Miss Moore describes a parakeet, in the poem entitled *My Apish Cousins:*

35

> *the parakeet,*
> *trivial and humdrum on examination,*
> *destroying*
> *bark and portions of the food it could not eat.*

There is also the legitimate field of purely descriptive poetry, with no general significance and no claim to any. For examples, one could cite many passages from *The Seasons,* or from Crabbe. There is no attempt in such poetry to communicate any feeling save the author's interest in visible beauties. Such poetry can scarcely rise to the greatest heights, but within its field it is sound, and it can, as in some of Crabbe's descriptions, especially of the sea, achieve surprising power. There is a good deal of this sort of thing scattered through English literature.

Growing out of these two types of poetry (that which refers to a genuine symbolic value, but implicitly, and the purely descriptive), there is a sentimental and more or less spurious variety, a good deal of which was recently fostered by the Imagist movement, but which actually antedates the Imagist movement by more than a century.

This poetry decribes landscape or other material, sometimes very ably, but assumes a quality or intensity of feeling of which the source is largely obscure. Thus in Collins' *Ode to Evening* we find a melancholy which at moments, as in the description of the bat, verges on disorder, and which at all times is far too profound to arise from an evening landscape alone. Collins' bat differs from Miss Moore's parakeet in this: that the parakeet is a genuine example of the way in which the exotic may become humdrum with familiarity—there is, in other words, a real perception of the bird involved, which does not exceed the order of experience which the bird may reasonably represent; whereas Collins' bat is not mad nor a sufficient motive for madness, but is used to express a state of mind irrelevant to him. It is as if a man should murder his mother, and then, to express his feelings, write an

Ode to Thunder. Or rather, it is as if a man should murder his mother with no consciousness of the act, but with all of the consequent suffering, and should then so express himself. A symbol is used to embody a feeling neither relevant to the symbol nor relevant to anything else of which the poet is conscious: the poet expresses his feeling as best he is able without understanding it. Collins in this poem, and in his odes to the disembodied passions, is perhaps the first purely romantic poet and one of the best. He does not, like Gray, retain amid his melancholy any of the classical gift for generalization, and he has provided the language with no familiar quotations. Shelley's *Ode to the West Wind,* and in a measure Keat's *Ode to the Nightingale,* are examples of the same procedure; namely, of expressing a feeling, not as among the traditional poets in terms of its motive, but in terms of something irrelevant or largely so, commonly landscape. No landscape, in itself, is an adequate motive for the feelings expressed in such poems as these; an appropriate landscape merely brings to mind certain feelings and is used as a symbol for their communication. The procedure can be defended on the grounds that the feeling may be universal and that the individual reader is at liberty to supply his own motive; but the procedure nevertheless does not make for so concentrated a poetry as the earlier method, and as an act of moral contemplation the poem is incomplete and may even be misleading and dangerous.

H. D. employs a formula nearly identical with that of Collins in most of her poems. In describing a Greek landscape, she frequently writes as if it had some intrinsic virtue automatically evoked by a perception of its qualities as landscape but more important than these qualities in themselves. It is not Greek history or civilization with which she is concerned, or most often it is not: the material is simple and more or less ideally bucolic. Frequently the ecstasy (the quality of feeling assumed is nearly identical in most of her poems) is evoked merely by rocks, sea, and islands. But it would not be evoked by any rock, sea, or islands: they must be Greek. But why must they be Greek? Because of Athenian civilization? If so, why the to-do about material irrelevant to Athenian civilization? There is some wholly obscure attachment on the poet's part to anything Greek, regardless of its value: the mention of anything Greek is sufficient to release her very intense feeling. But since the relationship between the feeling and the Greek landscape has no comprehensible source and is very strong, one must call it sentimental.

This is not to say that all her poetry is spoiled by it: much of it is spoiled and nearly all is tainted, but the taint is sometimes very slight; and the description, in addition, is sometimes very fine. Exotic landscapes of one kind or another have been employed in exactly this fashion for about a century, and, in America, the American landscape has been so employed by such writers as Whitman, Sandburg, Crane, and Williams.

6. *Explicit Reference to a non-existent or obscure principle of motivation.* This may at times be hard to distinguish from almost any of the types of obscurity which I have described, but there are to be found occasionally passages of pseudo-reference which will fit into scarcely any other category. Bearing in mind the fundamental obscurity of *The Dance,* by Hart Crane, an obscurity which I have already discussed at some length, let us consider these two lines from it:

> *Mythical brows we saw retiring—loth,*
> *Disturbed, and destined, into denser green.*

This passage depends for its effect wholly upon the feeling of motivation.

The mythical has rational content for the believer in myths or for him who can find an idea embodied in the myth. The major Greek divinities exist for us chiefly as allegorical embodiments of more or less Platonic ideas. What myths have we in mind here? None. Or none unless it be the myth of Pocahontas, which, as

38

we have seen, is irreducible to any idea. There is merely a feeling of mythicalness.

Loth, disturbed, destined are words of motivation; that is, each one implies a motive. But the nature of the motive is not given in the poem, nor is it deducible from the poem nor from the body of Crane's work. In fact, it is much easier to read some sort of general meaning into these lines in isolation than in their context, which has already been discussed.

Such terms give, then, a feeling of reasonable motivation unreasonably obscured. The poet speaks as if he had knowledge incommunicable to us, but of which he is able to communicate the resultant feelings. There is a feeling of mystery back of an emotion which the poet endeavors to render with precision. It is a skillful indulgence in irresponsibility. The skill is admirable, but not the irresponsibility. The poetry has a ghostly quality, as if it were only half there.

7. *Reference to a purely prvate symbolic value.* A poet, sometimes because of the limitations of his education, and sometimes for other reasons, may center his feelings in symbols shared with no one, or perhaps only with a small group. The private symbol may or may not refer to a clear concept or understanding. If it does so refer and the poetry is otherwise good, readers are likely eventually to familiarize themselves with the symbols; in fact brilliant writing alone will suffice to this end, as witness the efforts that have been made to clarify the essentially obscure concepts of Blake and of Yeats. A certain amount of this kind of thing, in fact, is probably inevitable in any poet, and sometimes, as in the references to private experience in the sonnets of Shakespeare, the obscurity, as a result of the accidents of history, can never be penetrated.

I have illustrated one extreme type of pseudo-reference with a passage from Ben Jonson; I might have utilized also the "mad songs" of the sixteenth and seventeenth centuries, such as were

39

written by Shakespeare, Fletcher, and Herrick. Samuel Johnson wrote thus in his *Life of Dryden:* "Dryden delighted to tread upon the brink of meaning, where light and darkness mingle. . . . This inclination sometimes produced nonsense, which he knew; and sometimes it issued in absurdity, of which perhaps he was not conscious." The method appears, then, to have been for a long time one of the recognized potentialities of poetic writing, but to have been more or less checked by the widespread command of rational subject matter.

It should naturally have been released, as it appears to have been, by a period of amateur mysticism, of inspiration for its own sake, by a tendency such as that which we have for some years past observed, to an increasingly great preoccupation with the fringe of consciousness, to an increasing emphasis on the concept of continuous experience, a tendency to identify, under the influence, perhaps, of scientific or of romantic monism, subconscious stimuli and reactions with occult inspiration, to confuse the divine and the visceral, and to employ in writing from such attitudes as this confusion might provide, a language previously reserved to the religious mystics. Such a change would involve along its way such indefinable philosophies as Bergsonism [1] and Transcendentalism,[2] such half-metaphorical sciences as psychoanalysis, and especially the popular myths and superstitions which they and the more reputable sciences have engendered. In such an intellectual milieu, semi-automatic writing begins to appear a legitimate and even a superior method.

Emerson, in *Merlin,* for example, gives this account of the bard's activity:

> *He shall not his brain encumber*
> *With the coil of rhythm and number;*

---

[1] *Le Bergsonisme,* by Julien Benda. Mercure de France: 1926. Also *Flux and Blur in Contemporary Art,* by John Crowe Ransom in the Sewanee Review, July, 1929.

[2] H. B. Parkes on Emerson, in the Hound and Horn, Summer, 1932.

But, leaving rule and pale forethought,
He shall aye climb
For his rhyme.
"Pass in, pass in," the angels say,
"In to the upper doors,
Nor count compartments of the floors,
But mount to paradise
By the stairway of surprise."

Just how much Emerson meant by this passage it would be hard to say; it is always hard to say just how much Emerson meant, and perhaps would have been hardest for Emerson. Mr. Tate reduces Emerson's Transcendentalism[1] to this formula: ". . . In Emerson, man is greater than any idea, and being the Over-Soul is potentially perfect; there is no struggle because—I state the Emersonian doctrine, which is very slippery, in its extreme terms —because there is no possibility of error. There is no drama in human character, because there is no tragic fault."

To continue with extreme terms—which will give us, if not what Emerson desired, the results which his doctrine and others similar have encouraged—we arrive at these conclusions: If there is no possibility of error, the revision of judgment is meaningless; immediate inspiration is correct; but immediate inspiration amounts to the same thing as unrevised reactions to stimuli; unrevised reactions are mechanical; man in a state of perfection is an automaton; an automatic man is insane. Hence, Emerson's perfect man is a madman.

The important thing about all this is not Emerson's originality, but his complete lack of any: exactly the same conclusions are deducible from the *Essay on Man,* and the convictions which lead to them one meets everywhere in the eighteenth, nineteenth, and twentieth centuries.

---

[1] *New England Culture and Emily Dickinson,* by Allen Tate: The Symposium, April, 1932.

41

Dr. W. C. Williams, for example, who, like Emerson, does not practice unreservedly what he preaches, but who more perhaps than any writer living encourages in his juniors a profound conviction of their natural rightness, a sentimental debauchery of self-indulgence, is able to write as follows: "It is the same thing you'll see in a brigand, a criminal of the grade of Gerald Chapman, some of the major industrial leaders, old-fashioned kings, the Norsemen, drunkards and the best poets. . . . Poetry is imposed on an age by men intent on something else, whose primary cleanliness of mind makes them automatically first-rate." [1]

A few months later Dr. Williams writes of and to his young admirers somewhat querulously: [2] "Instead of that—Lord how serious it sounds—let's play tiddly-winks with the syllables. . . . Experiment we must have, but it seems to me that a number of the younger writers has forgotten that writing doesn't mean just inventing new ways to say 'So's your Old Man.' I swear I myself can't make out for the life of me what many of them are talking about, and I have a will to understand them that they will not find in many another." He demands substance, not realizing that his own teachings have done their very respectable bit toward cutting the young men off from any.

The Emersonian and allied doctrines differ in their moral implications very little from any form of Quietism or even from the more respectable and Catholic forms of mysticism. If we add to the doctrine the belief in pantheism—that is, the belief that the Over-Soul is the Universe, that body and soul are one—we have the basis for the more or less Freudian mysticism of the surrealistes and such of their disciples as Eugene Jolas; we have also —probably—a rough notion of Hart Crane's mysticism. There is the danger for the Quietist that the promptings of the Devil or

---

[1] Blues (published by C. H. Ford, at Columbus, Miss.) for May, 1929.
[2] Blues for Autumn of 1930. The reference to the game of tiddly-winks will be clear only to those persons familiar with the imitators of Mr. James Joyce's fourth prose work, exclusive of *Exiles,* entitled at present *Work in Progress.*

of the viscera may be mistaken for the promptings of God. The pantheistic mystic identifies God, Devil, and viscera as a point of doctrine: he is more interested in the promptings of the "subconscious" mind than of the conscious, in the half-grasped intention, in the fleeting relationship, than in that which is wholly understood. He is interested in getting just as far off in the direction of the uncontrolled, the meaningless, as he can possibly get and still have the pleasure of talking about it. He is frequently more interested in the psychology of sleeping than in the psychology of waking;[1] he would if he could devote himself to exploring that realm of experience which he shares with sea-anemones, cabbages, and onions, in preference to exploring the realm of experience shared specifically with men.

So far as my own perceptions are able to guide me, it appears that the writers employing such methods are writing a little too much as Jonson's alchemists spoke, with a philosophical background insusceptible of definition, despite their apparently careful references to it, but as their own dupes, not to dupe others. They have revised Baudelaire's dictum that the poet should be the hypnotist and somnambulist combined; he should now be the cozener and the cozened. Crane, despite his genius, and the same is true of Mr. James Joyce, appears to answer Ben Jonson's scoundrels across the centuries, and in their own language, but like a somnambulist under their control.

This kind of writing is not a "new kind of poetry," as it has been called perennially since Verlaine discovered it in Rimbaud. It is the old kind of poetry with half the meaning removed. Its strangeness comes from its thinness. Indubitable genius has been expended upon poetry of this type, and much of the poetry so written will more than likely have a long life, and quite justly,

---

[1] Cf. Mr. James Joyce's *Work in Progress* which has appeared largely in the magazine Transition, published by Eugene Jolas, in Paris, and the voluminous works in practically every issue of that magazine by Mr. Joyce's apologists and imitators.

43

but the nature of the poetry should be recognized: it can do us no good to be the dupes of men who do not understand themselves.

TYPE V: QUALITATIVE PROGRESSION

The term *qualitative progression* I am borrowing from Mr. Kenneth Burke's volume of criticism, *Counterstatement,* to which I have already had several occasions to refer. This method arises from the same attitudes as the last, and it resembles the last except that it makes no attempt whatever at a rational progression. Mr. Pound's *Cantos* [1] are the perfect example of the form; they make no unfulfilled claims to matter not in the poetry, or at any rate relatively few and slight claims. Mr. Pound proceeds from image to image wholly through the coherence of feeling: his sole principle of unity is mood, carefully established and varied. That is, each statement he makes is reasonable in itself, but the progression from statement to statement is not reasonable: it is the progression either of random conversation or of revery. This kind of progression might be based upon an implicit rationality; in such a case the rationality of the progression becomes clearly evident before the poem has gone very far and is never thereafter lost sight of; in a poem of any length such implicit rationality would have to be supported by explicit exposition. But in Mr. Pound's poem I can find few implicit themes of any great clarity, and fewer still that are explicit.[2]

---

[1] *A Draft of XXX Cantos,* by Ezra Pound. Hours Press: 15 rue Guénégaud: Paris: 1930.

[2] Mr. Pound, writing in The New English Weekly, Vol. III, No. 4, of remarks similar to the above which I published in The Hound and Horn for the Spring of 1933, states: "I am convinced that one should not as a general rule reply to critics or defend works in process of being written. On the other hand, if one prints fragments of a work one perhaps owes the benevolent reader enough explanation to prevent his wasting time in unnecessary misunderstanding.

"The nadir of solemn and elaborate imbecility is reached by Mr. Winters in an American publication where he deplores my 'abandonment of logic in the Cantos,' presumably because he has never read my prose criticism and has never heard of the ideographic method, and thinks logic is limited to a few 'forms of

The principle of selection being less definite, the selection of details is presumably less rigid, though many of the details display a fine quality. The symbolic range is therefore reduced, since the form reduces the importance of selectiveness, or self-directed action. The movement is proportionately slow and wavering—indeed is frequently shuffling and undistinguished—and the range of material handled is limited: I do not mean that the poetry cannot refer to a great many types of actions and persons, but that it can find in them little variety of value—it refers to them all in the same way, that is, casually. Mr. Pound resembles a village loafer who sees much and understands little.

The following passage, however, the opening of the fourth *Canto,* illustrates this kind of poetry at its best:

Palace in smoky light,
Troy but a heap of smouldering boundary stones,
ANAXIFORMINGES! Aurunculeia!
Hear me. Cadmus of Golden Prows!
The silver mirrors catch the bright stones and flare,
Dawn, to our waking, drifts in the cool green light;
Dew-haze blurs, in the grass, pale ankles moving.
Beat, beat, whirr, thud, in the soft turf under the apple-trees,
Choros nympharum, goat-foot, with the pale foot alternate;
Crescent of blue-shot waters, green-gold in the shallows,
A black cock crows in the sea-foam;

---

logic' which better minds were already finding inadequate to the mental needs of the XIIIth century."

As to the particular defects of scholarship which Mr. Pound attributes to me, he is, alas, mistaken. For the rest, one may only say that civilization rests on the recognition that language possesses both connotative and denotative powers; that the abandonment of one in a poem impoverishes the poem to that extent; and that the abandonment of the denotative, or rational, in particular, and in a pure state, results in one's losing the only means available for checking up on the qualitative or "ideographic" sequences to see if they really are coherent in more than vague feeling. Mr. Pound, in other words, has no way of knowing whether he can think or not.

And by the curved, carved foot of the couch, claw-foot and
                              lion-head, an old man seated
Speaking in the low drone. . . . :
                              Ityn
Et ter flebiliter, Ityn, Ityn!
And she went toward the window and cast her down
          "And the while, the while swallows crying:
Ityn!

          "It is Cabestan's heart in the dish."
          "It is Cabestan's heart in the dish?
          "No other taste shall change this."

The loveliness of such poetry appears to me indubitable, but it is
merely a blur of revery: its tenuity becomes apparent if one compares it, for example, to the poetry of Paul Valéry, which achieves
effects of imagery, particularly of atmospheric imagery, quite as
extraordinary, along with precision, depth of meaning, and the
power that comes of close and inalterable organization, and,
though Mr. Pound's admirers have given him a great name as
a metrist, with incomparably finer effects of sound.

Mr. Kenneth Burke defines the qualitative progression [1] by
means of a very fine analysis of the preparation for the ghost in
Hamlet and by reference to the porter scene in *Macbeth,* and
then proceeds to the public house scene in *The Waste Land* [2] as
if it were equally valid. Actually, the qualitative progression in
Shakespeare is peripheral, the central movement of each play
being dependent upon what Mr. Burke calls the psychology of
the hero, or narrative logic, and so firmly dependent that occasional excursions into the rationally irrelevant can be managed
with no loss of force, whereas in *The Waste Land* the qualitative
progression is central: it is as if we should have a dislocated
series of scenes from *Hamlet* without the prince himself, or with

---

[1] *Counterstatement:* page 38 and thereafter.
[2] *Poems 1909-25,* by T. S. Eliot.

46

too slight an account of his history for his presence to be helpful. The difference between Mr. Eliot and Mr. Pound is this: that in *The Waste Land,* the prince is briefly introduced in the footnotes, whereas it is to be doubted that Mr. Pound could manage such an introduction were he so inclined. And the allegorical interpretation, or the germ of one, which Mr. Eliot has provided helps very little in the organization of the poem itself. To guess that the rain has a certain allegorical meaning when the rain is so indifferently described, or to guess at the allegorical relationships as a scholar might guess at the connections between a dozen odd pages recovered from a lost folio, is of very small aid to ourselves or to the poet.

If Mr. Eliot and Mr. Pound have employed conventions that can be likened to revery or to random conversation, Rimbaud and Mr. Joyce have gone farther. I quote Rimbaud's *Larme:*

> *Loin des oiseaux, des troupeaux, des villageoises,*
> *Je buvais accroupi dans quelque bruyère*
> *Entourée de tendres bois de noisetiers,*
> *Par un brouillard d'après-midi tiède et vert.*
>
> *Que pouvais-je boire dans cette jeune Oise,*
> *Ormeaux sans voix, gazon sans fleurs, ciel couvert:*
> *Que tirais-je à la gourde de colocase?*
> *Quelque liqueur d'or, fade et qui fait suer.*
>
> *Tel j'eusse été mauvaise enseigne d'auberge.*
> *Puis l'orage changea le ciel jusqu' au soir.*
> *Ce furent des pays noirs, des lacs, des perches,*
> *Des colonnades sous la nuit bleue, des gares.*
>
> *L'eau des bois se perdait sur les sables vierges.*
> *Le vent, du ciel, jetait des glaçons aux mares . . .*
> *Or! tel qu'un pêcheur d'or ou de coquillages,*
> *Dire que je n'ai pas eu souci de boire!*

47

The feelings of this poem are perhaps those attendant upon dream, delirium, or insanity. The coming of night and the storm is an intensification of the mood; the protagonist is suddenly sucked deeper in the direction of complete unconsciousness, and the terror becomes more profound.

In Mr. Joyce's latest work, at this time unfinished and without a title, but the work immediately subsequent to *Ulysses,* the dream convention is unmistakeable. It penetrates the entire texture of the work, not only the syntax but the words themselves, which are broken down and recombined in surprising ways.

This unbalance of the reasonable and the non-reasonable, whether the non-reason be of the type which I am now discussing or of the pseudo-referent type, is a vice wherever it occurs, and in the experimental writers who have worked very far in this direction, it is, along with Laforguian irony, which I shall discuss separately, one of the two most significant vices of style now flourishing. The reasons have already been mentioned here and there, but I shall summarize them.

Since only one aspect of language, the connotative, is being utilized, less can be said in a given number of words than if the denotative aspect were being fully utilized at the same time. The convention thus tends to diffuseness. Further, when the denotative power of language is impaired, the connotative becomes proportionately parasitic upon denotations in previous contexts, for words cannot have associations without meanings; and if the denotative power of language could be wholly eliminated, the connotative would be eliminated at the same stroke, for it is the nature of associations that they are associated with something. This means that non-rational writing, far from requiring greater literary independence than the traditional modes, encourages a quality of writing that is relatively derivative and insecure.

Since one of the means to coherence, or form, is impaired, form itself is enfeebled. In so far as form is enfeebled, precision of detail is enfeebled, for details receive precision from the structure

48

in which they function just as they may be employed to give that structure precision; to say that detail is enfeebled is to say that the power of discrimination is enfeebled. Mr. Joyce's new prose has sensitivity, for Mr. Joyce is a man of genius, but it is the sensitivity of a plasmodium, in which every cell squirms independently though much like every other. This statement is a very slight exaggeration if certain chapters are considered, notably the chapter entitled *Anna Livia Plurabelle,* but for the greater part it is no exaggeration.

The procedure leads to indiscriminateness at every turn. Mr. Joyce endeavors to express disintegration by breaking down his form, by experiencing disintegration before our very eyes, but this destroys much of his power of expression. Of course he controls the extent to which he impairs his form, but this merely means that he is willing to sacrifice just so much power of expression—in an effort to express something—and no more. He is like Whitman trying to express a loose America by writing loose poetry. This fallacy, the fallacy of expressive, or imitative, form, recurs constantly in modern literature.

Anna Livia Plurabelle is in a sense a modern equivalent of Gray's *Elegy,* one in which the form is expressive of the theme to an unfortunate extent; it blurs the values of all experience in the fact of change, and is unable, because of its inability to deal with rational experience, to distinguish between village Cromwells and the real article, between Othello on the one hand and on the other hand Shem and Shaun. It leads to the unlimited subdivision of feelings into sensory details till perception is lost, instead of to the summary and ordering of perception; it leads to disorganization and unintelligence. In Mr. Joyce we may observe the decay of genius. To the form of decay his genius lends a beguiling iridescence, and to his genius the decay lends a quality of novelty, which endanger the literature of our time by rendering decay attractive.

Mr. T. S. Eliot, in his introduction to the *Anabase* of St. Jean

Perse,[1] has written: "There is a logic of the imagination as well as a logic of concepts. People who do not appreciate poetry always find it difficult to distinguish between order and chaos in the arrangement of images." Later in the same essay he says: "I believe that this is a piece of writing of the same importance as the later work of Mr. James Joyce, as valuable as *Anna Livia Plurabelle*. And this is a high estimate indeed."

The logic in the arrangement of images of which Mr. Eliot speaks either is formulable, is not formulable, or is formulated. If it is neither formulated nor formulable (and he admits that it is not formulated), the word *logic* is used figuratively, to indicate qualitative progression, and the figure is one which it is hard to pardon a professed classicist for using at the present time. If the logic is formulable, there is no need for an apology and there is no excuse for the reference to *Anna Livia Plurabelle;* and there is reason to wonder why no formulation is given or suggested by the critic. Mr. Eliot has reference obviously, merely to the type of graduated progression of feeling that we have been discussing, and the poem shares the weakness of other works already discussed.

Mr. Eliot's remarks are typical of the evasive dallying practiced by the greater number of even the most lucid and reactionary critics of our time when dealing with a practical problem of criticism. It is well enough to defend Christian morality and to speak of tradition, but forms must be defined and recognized or the darkness remains. A classicist may admire the sensibilities of Joyce and Perse with perfect consistency (though beyond a certain point not with perfect taste), but he cannot with consistency justify the forms which those sensibilities have taken.

If the reader is curious to compare with the *Anabase* a prose work of comparable length and subject in the traditional manner, he will find a specimen of the highest merit in *The Destruction*

---

[1] *Anabasis,* a poem by St. Jean Perse, with translation and Preface by T. S. Eliot. Faber and Faber, London: 1930.

of *Tenochtitlan* [1] by William Carlos Williams, which, like the *Anabase*, deals with the military conquest of an exotic nation, but which utilizes not only qualitative progression but every other mode proper to narrative and in a masterly way. The form is exact; the rhetoric is varied and powerful; the details, unlike those of the *Anabase,* are exact both as description and, where symbolic force is intended, as symbols. Displaying fullness and precision of meaning, it is in no wise "strange" and has been ignored. But its heroic prose is superior to the prose of *Anabase* and of *Anna Livia Plurabelle,* is superior in all likelihood to nearly any other prose of our time and to most of the verse.

The so-called stream-of-consciousness convention of the contemporary novel is a form of qualitative progression. It may or may not be used to reveal a plot, but at best the revelation can be fragmentary since the convention excludes certain important functions of prose—summary, whether narrative or expository, being the chief. It approximates the manner of the chain of thought as it might be imagined in the mind of the protagonist: that is, it tends away from the reconsidered, the revised, and tends toward the fallacy of imitative form, which I have remarked in the work of Joyce and of Whitman.[2] It emphasizes, wittingly or not, abject imitation at the expense of art; it is technically naturalism; it emphasizes to the last degree the psychology of the hero, but the least interesting aspect of it, the accidental. Mr. Kenneth Burke, in his novel, *Toward a Better Life* [3] thus

---

[1] *In the American Grain,* by W. C. Williams. A. and C. Boni, New York, 1925.

[2] This law of literary æsthetics has never that I know been stated explicitly. It might be thus formulated: Form is expressive invariably of the state of mind of the author; a state of formlessness is legitimate subject matter for literature, and in fact all subject matter, as such, is relatively formless; but the author must endeavor to give form, or meaning, to the formless—in so far as he endeavors that his own state of mind may imitate or approximate the condition of the matter, he is surrendering to the matter instead of mastering it. Form, in so far as it endeavors to imitate the formless, destroys itself.

[3] Op. Cit.

51

falls into the very pit which he has labored most diligently to avoid: he expands his entire rhetorical energy on his sentences, but lets his story run loosely through the mind of his hero. The quality of the detail is expository and aphoristic; the structure is not expository but is qualitative. One feels a discrepancy between the detail and the form; the detail appears labored, the form careless and confused.

The convention of reminiscence, a form of the stream-of-consciousness technique, which is employed by Mr. Burke and by others, has a defect peculiar to itself alone. It commonly involves the assumption, at the beginning of a story, of the state of feeling proper to the conclusion; then by means of revelation, detail by detail, the feeling is justified. In other words, the initial situations are befogged by unexplained feeling, and the feeling does not develop in a clean relationship to the events. The result is usually a kind of diffuse lyricism.

TYPE VI: THE ALTERNATION OF METHOD

Two or more methods may be used in formal arrangements. In a play or novel, where there is plenty of room for change, a great many modes of procedure may be employed. In a lyrical poem there will seldom be more than two. In Marvell's *To His Coy Mistress,* for example, the progression from stanza to stanza is logical, but within each stanza the progression is repetitive.

Mallarmé's *L'Après-Midi d'un Faune* illustrates a method toward which various writers have tended; namely to shift out of the logical into the pseudo-referent or qualitative, back into the logical, and so on, but at irregular intervals. The appearance of shifting may be due, of course, to my own inability to follow the argument, but it appears to be a real shifting. The faun recounts his adventure, trying to philosophize concerning it: hence narrative alternates with what should be exposition, but actually both narrative and exposition move in a more or less dreamy fashion at times, so that the cleavage in method does not coincide with the cleavage in subject matter.

A short poem or passage may be composed of alternating passages of two distinct and more or less opposed types of feeling, or of two types of feeling combined and without discernible alternation. A long poem may involve many types of feeling, but where two types alone are involved, one of them is usually ironic: it is with this situation in particular that I am here concerned. Byron, for example, commonly builds up a somewhat grandiloquent effect only to demolish it by ridicule or by ludicrous anticlimax. His effects are crude in the main, the poems being ill-written, but he was the first poet to embody on a pretentious scale, and to popularize, this common modern attitude.

The particular form which his method has taken in modern poetry is closely related to the poetry of Jules Laforgue, though Laforgue is not in every case an influence. I quote Laforgue's *Complainte du Printemps:*

> *Permettez, ô sirène,*
> *Voici que votre haleine*
> *Embaume la verveine;*
> *C'est le printemps qui s'amène!*

—Ce système, en effet, ramène le printemps,
Avec son impudent cortège d'excitants.

> *Otez donc ces mitaines;*
> *Et n'ayez, inhumaine,*
> *Que mes soupirs pour traine:*
> *Ous'qu'il y a de la gêne . . .*

—Ah! yeux bleus méditant sur l'ennui de leur art!
Et vous, jeunes divins, aux soirs crus de hasard!

53

Du géant à la naine,
Vois, tout bon sire entraine
Quelque contemporaine,
Prendre l'air, par hygiène . . .

—Mais vous saignez ainsi pour l'amour de l'exil!
Pour l'amour de l'Amour! D'ailleurs, ainsi soit-il . . .

T'ai-je fait de la peine?
Oh! viens vers les fontaines
Où tournent les phalènes
Des nuits Elyséennes!

—Pimbèche aux yeux vaincus, bellâtre aux beaux jarrets,
Donnez votre fumier à la fleur du Regret.

Voilà que son haleine
N'embaum' plus la verveine!
Drôle de phénomène . . .
Hein, à l'année prochaine?

Vierges d'hier, ce soir traineuses de fœtus,
A genoux! voici l'heure où se plaint l'Angélus.

Nous n'irons plus au bois,
Les pins sont éternels,
Les cors ont des appels! . . .
Neiges des pâles mois,
Vous serez mon missel!
—Jusqu'au jour du dégel.

The opposition and cancellation of the two moods is so obvious as to need no particular comment: there is romantic nostalgia (romantic because it has no discernible object, is a form of un-motivated feeling) canceled by an immature irony (immature because it depends upon the obviously but insignificantly ridiculous, as in the third quatrain, or upon a kind of physical detail which is likely to cause pain to the adolescent but which is not likely to interest the mature, as in couplets four and five). The application of the irony, in turn, deepens the nostalgia, as in the fourth quatrain and the conclusion. It is the formula for adolescent disillusionment: the unhappily "cynical" reaction to the loss of a feeling not worth having.

A few years earlier than Laforgue, Tristan Corbière had employed the same procedure in a few poems, most vigorously in *Un Jeune Qui S'en Va,* but from his greatest work (*La Rapsode Foraine* and *Cris d'Aveugle,* two poems which are probably superior to any French verse of the nineteenth century save the best of Baudelaire), it is either absent or has lost itself amid an extremely complex cluster of feelings.

Previously to Corbière, Gautier had written in much the same fashion, but usually of very different subjects. His *Nostalgies des Obélisques* are examples. They consist of two poems, monologues spoken by two Egyptian obelisks, one of which has been transported to Paris and compares the Parisian and Egyptian scenes, lamenting the loss of the latter, the other of which remains behind, only to make the same comparison but to long for Paris. The alternations are almost mathematically balanced, though occasionally both moods will rest on a single image, as when an Egyptian animal performs a grotesquely ludicrous action in magnificent language. There is not, in Gautier, the adolescent mood of Laforgue, for Gautier was a vastly abler rhetorician and was too astute to give way to such a mood, but there is no meaning to his experience, as it appears in such poems, outside of the contrast, and the contrast is painfully precise. Gautier resembles a child fascinated by the task of separating and arranging exactly, blocks of exactly two colors. The moral sense of such a poet is too simple to hold the interest for many readings. Mr. Eliot in his quatrains employed the same formula; in fact several of his most striking lines are translated or imitated from *Emaux et Camées.*[1]

Similar to Laforgue's use of this kind of irony is Mr. Pound's use of it in *Hugh Selwyn Mauberly.*[2] The two attitudes at variance in this sequence are a nostalgic longing of which the visible object is the society of the Pre-Raphaelites and of the related poets of the nineties, and a compensatory irony which admits the mediocrity of that society or which at least ridicules its mediocre aspects. Even in the midst of the most biting comment, the yearning is unabated:

> *The Burne-Jones cartons*
> *Have preserved her eyes;*
> *Still, at the Tate, they teach*
> *Cophetua to rhapsodize;*
>
> *Thin, like brook-water,*
> *With a vacant gaze.*
> *The English Rubaiyat was still-born*
> *In those days.*[3]

And again, to quote an entire poem:

> *Among the pickled foetuses and bottled bones*
> *Engaged in perfecting the catalogue,*
> *I found the last scion of the*
> *Senatorial families of Strassbourg, Monsieur Verog.*
>
> *For two hours he talked of Gallifet;*
> *Of Dowson; Of the Rhymers' Club;*
> *Told me how Johnson (Lionel) died*
> *By falling from a high stool in a pub . . .*

---

[1] Poems 1909-25, by T. S. Eliot: the series of poems in octosyllabic quatrains, of which the most successful is *Sweeney among the Nightingales.*

[2] *Hugh Selwyn Mauberly*, by Ezra Pound. Included in *Personae*, by Ezra Pound. Boni and Liveright. New York. 1926.

[3] *Yeux Glauges*, from *Mauberly.*

But showed no trace of alcohol
At the autopsy, privately performed—
Tissues preserved—the pure mind
Arose toward Newman as the whiskey warmed.

Dowson found harlots cheaper than hotels;
Headlam for uplift; Image impartially imbued
With raptures for Bacchus, Terpsichore, and the Church
So spoke the author of "The Dorian Mood,"

M. Verog, out of step with the decade,
Detached from his contemporaries,
Neglected by the young,
Because of these reveries.[1]

As so often happens when this kind of irony occurs, the poem is guilty of a certain amount both of doggerel and of verbosity. It is not without virtues, however; and it is not the best poem in the sequence. It is worth noting that the two moods are not precisely separable here, as in so much of Eliot and of Gautier, but are usually coincident. This likewise is true of the irony of Wallace Stevens.

Mr. Stevens' commonest method of ironic comment is to parody his own style, with respect to its slight affectation of elegance; or perhaps it were more accurate to say that this affectation itself is a parody, however slight, of the purity of his style in its best moments. The parody frequently involves an excess of alliteration, as in the opening lines of the poem entitled *Of the Manner of Addressing Clouds:*[2]

Gloomy grammarians in golden gowns,
Meekly you keep the mortal rendezvous. . . .

---

[1] *"Siena Mi Fe': Disfecemi Maremma."* the same.
[2] This poem and others by the same author may be found in: *Harmonium,* by Wallace Stevens, Alfred A. Knopf, New York, 1931.

The same device is more obviously employed in *The Comedian as the Letter C,* in which appears an explicit statement of the source of the irony, his inability to justify the practice of his art, his own lack of respect for what he is doing, and in which the irony frequently descends to the tawdry. In some poems he is entirely free of the quality, as, for examples, in *Sunday Morning, Death of a Soldier, Of Heaven Considered as a Tomb.* In such work, and in those poems such as that last quoted and, to choose a more ambitious example, *Le Monocle de Mon Oncle,* in which the admixture is very slight, he is probably the greatest poet of his generation.

The double mood is not strictly post-romantic, either in English or in French, nor is ironic poetry, but both are perhaps more frequently so, and in pre-romantic poetry neither is employed for the purpose which I have been describing. For instance, in Dryden's *MacFlecknoe,* the combination of the heroic style and the satirical intention constitutes a kind of double mood, but there is no mutual cancellation; the same is true of Pope's *Dunciad,* of *La Pucelle* by Voltaire, and of a good many other poems. Churchill's *Dedication to Warburton,* in its semblance of eulogy actually covering a very bitter attack, employs both irony (as distinct from satire) and something that might be called a double mood. But in all of these examples, the poet is perfectly secure in his own feelings; he is attacking something or someone else from a point of view which he regards as tenable. The essence of romantic irony, on the other hand, is this: that the poet ridicules himself for a kind or degree of feeling which he can neither approve nor control; so that the irony is simply the act of confessing a state of moral insecurity which the poet sees no way to improve.[1]

A twentieth century ironist who resembles the earlier ironists

---

[1] The relationship and partial indebtedness of this technical analysis of romantic irony to Irving Babbitt's more general treatment of the same subject in *Rousseau and Romanticism* will be evident to anyone familiar with the latter.

instead of her contemporaries is Miss Marianne Moore. If one can trust the evidence of her earlier and shorter poems, she stems from the early Elizabethan epigrammatists. Turberville, a few years before Spenser and Sidney, writes *To One of Little Wit*:

> *I thee advise*
> *If thou be wise*
> *To keep thy wit*
> *Though it be small.*
> *'Tis hard to get*
> *And far to fet—*
> *'Twas ever yet*
> *Dear'st ware of all.*

Miss Moore writes *To an Intramural Rat*: [1]

> *You make me think of many men*
> *Once met, to be forgot again,*
> *Or merely resurrected*
> *In a parenthesis of wit*
> *That found them hastening through it*
> *Too brisk to be inspected.*

In Miss Moore's later work, the same quality is developed through a very elaborate structure, in which the magnificent and the curious are combined with the ironical and the ludicrous: I have in mind in particular such poems as *My Apish Cousins* (later entitled *The Monkeys*), *New York, A Grave, and Black Earth*. These poems illustrate perfectly Miss Moore's virtues: unshakeable certainty of intention, a diction at once magnificent and ironic (her cat, for example, in *My Apish Cousins*, raises Gautier's formula for fantastic zoölogy into the realm of high art), and the fairly consistent control of an elaborate rhetoric. They suggest her weaknesses, which are more evident in other

---

[1] *Obervations*, by Marianne Moore, The Dial Press, New York, 1924.

poems: a tendency to a rhetoric more complex than her matter, a tendency to be led astray by opportunities for description, and a tendency to base her security on a view of manners instead of morals.

The romantic antithesis of moods is the central theme of Joyce's *Ulysses,* which, at the same time, is rendered diffuse by a stream-of-consciousness technique and by the fallacy of imitative form.[1] The book has great virtues, which its admirers have long since fully enumerated, but it lacks final precision both of form and of feeling. It is adolescent as Laforgue is adolescent; it is ironic about feelings which are not worth the irony.

Mr. Kenneth Burke's novel, *Towards a Better Life,* displays the same kind of irony, which adds to the confusion coming from other sources which I have already mentioned. Mr. Burke, instead of giving us the progression of a narrative, endeavors, as I have said, to give us a progression of pure feeling. Frequently there is not even progression; we have merely a repetitious series of Laforguian antitheses.

Mr. Burke, in his volume of criticism, *Counterstatement,* offers the best defense with which I am familiar, of the attitudes to which I am now objecting.[2] He writes: "The ironist is essentially *impure,* even in the chemical sense of purity, since he is divided. He must deprecate his own enthusiasms, and distrust his own resentments. He will unite waveringly, as the components of his attitude, 'dignity, repugnance, the problematical, and art.' To the slogan-minded, the ralliers about a flag, the marchers who convert a simple idea into a simple action, he is an 'outsider.' Yet he must observe them with nostalgia, he must feel a kind of awe for their fertile assurance, even while remaining on the alert to stifle it with irony each time he discovers it growing in unsuspected quarters within himself."

---

[1] *Ulysses,* by James Joyce, Shakespeare and Co., Paris.
[2] In the essay on *Thomas Mann and André Gide,* pages 116 and following.

In admitting no distinction save that between the ironist and the slogan-minded, Mr. Burke himself verges upon a dangerous enthusiasm, perhaps even upon a slogan. The whole issue comes down to the question of how carefully one is willing to scrutinize his feelings and correct them. Miss Rowena Lockett once remarked to me that Laforgue resembles a person who speaks with undue harshness and then apologizes; whereas he should have made the necessary subtractions before speaking. The objection implies an attitude more sceptical and cautious than that of Mr. Burke; instead of irony as the remedy for the unsatisfactory feeling, it recommends the waste-basket and a new beginning. And this recommendation has its basis not only in morality but in æsthetics: the romantic ironists whom I have cited write imperfectly in proportion to their irony; their attitude, which is a corruption of feeling, entails a corruption of style—that is, the irony is an admission of careless feeling, which is to say careless writing, and the stylist is weak in proportion to the grounds for his irony. To see this, one has only to compare the best work of these writers to the best of Churchill, Pope, Gay, Marot, or Voltaire.

Mr. Burke states elsewhere: [1] "The 'sum total of art' relieves the artist of the need of seeing life steadily and seeing it whole. He will presumably desire to be as comprehensive as he can, but what he lacks in adjustability can be supplied by another artist affirming some other pattern with equal conviction."

Except for the likelihood that two opposite excesses may not be equivalent to something intelligent, Mr. Burke's statement may up to a certain point be well enough for Society (whatever the word may mean in this connection), but from the standpoint of the individual seeking to train himself, it is not very helpful.

Mr. Burke does give the artist a morality, however: he bases it upon what he believes Society needs: "Alignment of forces. On the side of the practical: efficiency, prosperity, material acquisi-

---

[1] *Counterstatement:* the chapter called *Lexicon Rhetoricæ:* page 231.

tions, increased consumption, 'new needs,' expansion, higher standards of living, progressive rather than regressive evolutions, in short ubiquitous optimism. . . . On the side of the æsthetic (the Bohemian): inefficiency, indolence, dissipation, vacillation, mockery, distrust, 'hypochondria,' non-conformity, bad sportsmanship, in short, negativism. We have here a summary of the basic notion of all of Mr. Burke's writings, the doctrine of balanced excesses. Perhaps they will balance each other, and perhaps not, but suppose a man should desire to be intelligent with regard to himself alone; suppose, in other words, a particular artist should lack entirely the high altruism which Mr. Burke demands of him—of what value will he find Mr. Burke's morality? Mr. Burke's doctrine, in the realms of art and of morality, is really the least sceptical, the most self-confident possible: no point of view is tenable and hence no feeling is adequately motivated; all feeling is thus seen to be excessive, and neither more nor less excessive than any other, for there is no standard of measurement; any excess can be cancelled by an opposite excess, which is automatically equal, and careful evaluation, as it is impossible, is likewise unnecessary.

I have stated the matter very baldly, but quite fairly. Any artist holding Mr. Burke's views, in so far as he is an artist, will be restrained more or less by his natural feeling for rightness of expression; but as the theory does not, if pushed to its conclusions, admit the existence of rightness, the theory encourages shoddy writing and shoddy living. The hero of Mr. Burke's novel goes mad, for the reason that, the need of judgment having been removed by his (and Mr. Burke's) theories, the power of judgment atrophies; yet Mr. Burke continues to preach the doctrine which brought him to this end.

The perfect embodiment of Mr. Burke's doctrines, whether as an individual man, or as an allegorical representation of Society, is that Shan O'Neale who flourished in Ireland in the sixteenth century, and whose character David Hume has described as fol-

62

lows in his *History of England:* "He was a man equally noted for his pride, his violence, his debaucheries, and his hatred of the English nation. He is said to have put some of his followers to death because they endeavored to introduce the use of bread after the English fashion. Though so violent an enemy to luxury, he was extremely addicted to riot; and was accustomed, after his intemperance had thrown him into a fever, to plunge his body into the mire, that he might allay the flame which he had raised by former excesses."

POETIC CONVENTION

I SHALL endeavor to define a concept which is fundamental to any discussion of poetry, and shall employ to indicate the concept the terms *convention* and *conventional*. In popular speech, these terms are frequently synonymous with *banality* and *banal;* in discussions of literary technique, the term *convention* frequently signifies *a fixed and generally accepted device for the simplified representation of some particular kind of truth,* as: the pastoral convention, the convention of the dramatic unities, the convention of the dramatic chorus. The sense in which I shall use the term is not unrelated to these, but it is none-the-less distinct from them. It is a sense which is perhaps more difficult to grasp, which also is frequently vaguely implicit in the use of the word for both of the above meanings.

It should be remembered in connection with this and other definitions that a critical term ordinarily indicates a quality, and not an objectively demonstrable entity, yet that every term in criticism is an abstraction, that is, in a sense, is statistical or quantitative in its own nature. This means that no critical term can possibly be more than a very general indication of the nature of a perception. Philosophy labors under the same difficulty, since all generalization is made from perception, or from experience inextricably involved in perception. There is nothing revolutionary about such a statement, but it needs to be kept in mind. Much of the Socratic hair-splitting of some of the more recent critics arises from a failure to observe in particular instances that any critical definition is merely an indication of a unique experience which cannot be exactly represented by any formula, though it may be roughly mapped out; and it is frequently of greater importance to discover something of the nature of the experience

64

than to reduce the more or less expert formula to something simpler and still less veracious and then to demolish it.

When one speaks of standards of critical judgment, one does not ordinarily think of weights and measures. One has in mind certain feelings of rightness and completeness, which have been formed in some measure, refined in a large measure, through a study of the masters. The terms that one will use as a critic will stand for those feelings. Definitions of such terms can never be exact beyond misconstruction, but by dint of careful description and the use of good examples, one may succeed in communicating standards with reasonable accuracy—to those, at least, to whom it is important that communication should be made. For if values cannot be measured, they can be judged; and the bare existence of both art and criticism shows the persistence of the conviction that accuracy of judgment is at least ideally possible, and that the best critics, despite the inevitable margin of difference, and despite their inevitable duller moments, approximate accuracy fairly closely: by that, I mean that great men tend to agree with each other, and the fact is worth taking seriously. I am more or less aware of the extent of the catalogue of disagreements that might be drawn up in reply to such a statement, but it is far less astounding than, let us say, the unanimity of the best minds on the subject of Homer and Vergil, particularly if we accept the doctrine of relativism with any great seriousness.

The two paragraphs foregoing are not to be regarded as a plea for intellectual amateurism or for any kind of impressionism. Definition should be as exact as possible, as professional as possible. It is through the definition of others that we learn of realms of perception that we have overlooked, and are brought to a position in which we may attempt judgment and perhaps arrive at approbation. But there are limits to language, and the failure to remember this fact, even though one may grant it readily as a formal proposition, can lead to nothing save incomprehension on the part of a reader and obscurantism on the part of a writer.

65

Keeping these warnings in mind, the reader is now requested to examine carefully the two poems following. The first is entitled *Eros* [1] and is by Robert Bridges; the second [2] has no title, and is by William Carlos Williams.

Why hast thou nothing in thy face?
Thou idol of the human race,
Thou tyrant of the human heart,
The flower of lovely youth that art;
Yea, and that standest in thy youth
An image of eternal truth,
With thy exuberant flesh so fair,
That only Pheidias might compare,
Ere from his chaste marmoreal form
Time had decayed the colors warm;
Like to his gods in thy proud dress
Thy starry sheen of nakedness.

Surely thy body is thy mind,
For in thy face is nought to find,
Only thy soft unchristened smile,
That shadows neither love nor guile,
But shameless will and power immense,
In secret sensuous innocence.

O king of joy, what is thy thought?
I dream thou knowest it is nought,
And wouldst in darkness come, but thou
Makest the light where'er thou go.
Ah, yet no victim of thy grace,
None who ere longed for thy embrace,
Hath cared to look upon thy face.

---

[1] *Shorter Poems,* by Robert Bridges. Oxford Press, 1931.
[2] *Spring and All,* by William Carlos Williams, Contact Publishing Company, Paris, 1923.

66

By the road to the contagious hospital
under the surge of the blue
mottled clouds driven from the
northeast—a cold wind. Beyond, the
waste of broad muddy fields
brown with dried weeds, standing and fallen

patches of standing water
the scattering of tall trees

All along the road the reddish
purplish, forked, upstanding, twiggy
stuff of bushes and small trees
with dead, brown leaves under them
leafless vines—

Lifeless in appearance, sluggish
dazed spring approaches—

They enter the new world naked,
cold, uncertain of all
save that they enter. All about them
the cold familiar wind—

Now the grass, tomorrow
the stiff curl of wildcarrot leaf

One by one objects are defined—
It quickens: clarity, outline of leaf

But now the stark dignity of
entrance—Still, the profound change
has come upon them: rooted they
grip down and begin to awaken.

A scrutiny of these poems will show that most of the poetic power is concentrated in less than half the number of the lines; in the first poem, the greatest power is reached in the middle paragraph, and in the second poem it is reached in the eight lines beginning *Lifeless in appearance*. The remaining lines in each poem vary in power; the chief virtue of many of the lines in each poem may seem at first glance to reside in the plain conveyance of necessary information.

And yet the first glance, if it has led to this conclusion, is illusory. The passages of the greatest power lose much of their power in isolation: therefore one is justified in saying that something essentially poetic suffuses the entire structure.

This "something" I shall name the *convention* of the poem: I shall use the term *convention* to indicate the initial assumption of feeling, or value, to which the poem is laying claim. It is not equivalent to the term *style,* though style is necessary to the establishment and maintenance of convention. Again, convention is distinct from any set of technical devices, though technical devices will be employed in the establishment of any convention. The convention of a poem is not, finally, a part or ingredient of a poem, for a poem is a unit, and the dissection of it is artificial, though frequently valuable if one recognize the nature of the process. Convention is an aspect of poetry that can best be explained by illustration.

Consider the opening lines of the poem by Williams. The nervous meter, words like "surge," "mottled," "driven," suggest an intensity of feeling not justified by the actual perceptions in the lines. These words are therefore conventional. The content of the passage is factual to a greater degree than it is perceptual, and in itself has extremely little interest. In thus describing the lines, I employ the terms *perception* and *perceptual* solely with reference to the awareness of the author of fine relationships between facts observed (or perceived directly) and language, or the medium of judgment and communication. More feeling is *assumed,* or *claimed,* by the poet, in a passage such as that under discussion, than is justified by his language: he claims more than he is able to communicate, or more, perhaps, than he chooses to

68

communicate. At first glance a passage of this sort appears a trifle strained, to use a common but somewhat vague epithet. But in the present poem, the strain is deliberately sought and exactly rendered. The tempo established in these lines, the whole quality of the feeling, the information conveyed, are all necessary to, in fact are a part of, the effect of the eight central lines. With the line beginning "lifeless in appearance" the intensity claimed by the opening is at once justified and increased by the quality of the perception: the initial assumption prepares one for the exact increase which occurs, and the preparation is necessary. The feeling of the last two of the eight central lines (*Now the grass,* etc.) differs widely from the feeling in the preceding six, but is dependent largely upon the feeling already established in the preceding six for its existence. The feeling is one of pathos, aroused by the small and familiar in austere and unfriendly surroundings. It is related to the feeling of *Animula Vagula.* The last six lines of Williams' poem revert to the conventional level, but carry with them, if read in their context, an echo of the precedent intensity.

My analysis of the poem has been oversimplified for the sake of momentary convenience. The conventional passages are not devoid of perceptual value: the skill with which the details of the landscape are placed in juxtaposition in the opening lines is in itself an act of perception. The beat, also, in lines nine, ten, and eleven, taken in conjunction with the material described, has perceptual value, and one could point out other details. The details are not of a uniform level of intensity: no two details can be so. The important thing for the moment is that the intensity claimed by the passage is on the whole in excess of the justification within the passage, and that the intensity assumed is indicated with the greatest of firmness, with the result that departures from it can be made with equal firmness.

For example, I have said that the beat in lines nine, ten, and eleven has perceptual value, as indicating the "twiggy" appearance of the landscape. Yet the meaning-content (as distinct from

69

the sound-content) of every adjective contributing to this perception is a little vague: "reddish," "purplish," for instance, are by definition uncertain in their import. But the vagueness is willed and controlled: one has a definite measure of vagueness set against the definite intensity of the meter. To make these perceptions more precise would lessen the impact of the central lines. This mastery of emphases and of the conventional is one of the marks, and probably the most important mark, of the great stylist: without this mastery poetry degenerates into slipshod sentiment at worst, and at best, as in much of Crane, into brilliant, but disconnected, epithets and ejaculations.

Conventional language, then, is not in itself stereotyped language, though a strongly defined convention may safely carry a little stereotyped language: in fact stereotyped language may often be used deliberately to establish a convention. Conventional language is not dead language, but rather is very subtly living, if well employed. In so far as any passage is purely conventional, that is, conventional as distinct from perceptual, it does not represent a perception of its own content, the feeling it assumes is not justified within the passage in question. When I speak of *conventional language,* I shall mean language in which the perceptual content is slight or negligible. A conventional passage, the adjective *conventional* being employed in this sense, is poetic, however, in so far as it is essential to the entire poetic intention, that is, in so far as its effect reaches forward or backward within the poem.

Let me resume my definitions briefly, that I may add a little more before proceeding. Poetic convention is the initial, or basic, assumption of feeling in any poem, from which all departures acquire their significance. The convention of a poem is present, or at least discernible as the norm of feeling, throughout the entire poem, so that in a sense all the language of a poem is conventional; but when I use the term *conventional language* I shall commonly be speaking of passages in which the perceptual justification of the feeling is slight. I shall likewise use the term con-

70

ventional in a generic sense, to indicate a type of convention, as: the Laforguian convention, the pseudo-referent convention. The context will ordinarily render my intention perfectly clear.

But I am concerned for the moment with the subject of specific convention, primarily. The conventional intensity in the poem by Williams was somewhat in excess of the perceptual value of many lines in the poem; it would, as I said, appear slightly strained to many readers. This feeling of strain is not necessarily concomitant with convention; in the poem by Bridges there is no such strain. The movement of Bridges' poem is quiet; the language, like that of Williams, is plain, but it verges more nearly on the stereo-typed than does the language of Williams in the poem quoted. The intensity assumed is at a more familiar level of initial assumption and so appears never to be in excess of the least important fact conveyed: that is, the convention is nearer to the matter-of-fact tone of prose than is the convention employed by Williams. Strangely enough, a convention of such a type can serve, as on this occasion, with perfect effectiveness in a poem of the most powerful feeling.

I shall now give a brief account of a few general terms deducible from these ideas regarding convention:

I. *Traditional poetry* is poetry which endeavors to utilize the greatest possible amount of the knowledge and wisdom, both technical and moral, but technical only in so far as it does not obstruct the moral, to be found in precedent poetry. It assumes the ideal existence of a normal quality of feeling, a normal convention, to which the convention of any particular poem should more or less conform. Actually, the conformity of any poem, even though the traditional norm could be exactly defined or could be found embodied in a single work (Lady Winchilsea's flawlessly beautiful and eminently traditional poems *The Tree* or *The Change,* or George Herbert's *Church Monuments*), would be impossible, since every poem, good or bad, is unique. But if we cannot lay a finger precisely upon the norm, we can recognize the more or less normal. If the reader does not follow me, let me point out that it is easy to recognize the Laforguian convention in Apollinaire, in the early Eliot, and in Pound's *Mauberly,* or the Miltonic convention, even though indifferently managed, in Thomson and in Wordsworth. The traditional norm is less obviously discernible, for it embraces a wider variety of essential qualities, and no one of them receives so marked an emphasis. One might describe it negatively as that type of poetry which displays at one and the same time the greatest possible distinction with the fewest possible characteristics recognizable as the marks of any particular school, period, or man; as, in brief, that type of poetry which displays the greatest polish of style and the smallest trace of mannerism. One may describe traditional poetry positively by saying that it possesses these closely related qualities: (1) equivalence of motivation and feeling; (2) a form that permits a wide range of feeling; (3) a conventional norm of feeling which makes for a minimum of "strain"; (4) a form and a convention which permit the extraction from every unit of language of its maximum content, both of connotation and of denotation; that is, a form and a convention which are in the highest degree economical, or efficient.

II. *Experimental poetry* endeavors to widen the racial experience, or to alter it, or to get away from it, by establishing abnormal conventions. In one sense or another Spenser, Donne, Milton, Hopkins, Laforgue, and Rimbaud are experimental poets of a very marked kind. The most striking example in English of a convention of heightened intensity (that is, of what the unsympathetic might call poetic strain) is to be found in *Paradise Lost.* When the poem does not achieve grandeur, it is grandiloquent; yet the quality of the grandiloquence could have been achieved only by a master of the highest order, and without it the poem could hardly have been accomplished. As an act of invention, of daring experiment, the creation of Miltonic blank verse, both

72

meter and rhetoric, is not equalled in English poetry; in fact one is tempted to wonder if it is equalled in any other. The perils amid which Milton ventured and which he avoided with perfect equanimity are best estimated by a consideration of his disciples. Yet in spite of his mastery, the emphatic and violent rhetoric which he created limits his range, as compared to the range of Shakespeare, a man of comparable genius but working in a series of conventions which are relatively traditional. The same relationship holds between the sonnets of the two men, and is the more readily discernible, perhaps, because of the smaller form. Milton is the more complex rhetorician, but the simpler moralist and a man of far less subtle perception. Milton is the nobler, but Milton's nobility is in part, and as compared to Shakespeare, the over-emphasis of imperception.

An experimental poet may be traditional in many aspects. Thus Crashaw, who carries certain experimental qualities of diction and image found in Donne much farther from the norm than even Donne ventured, is nevertheless traditional in that he utilizes by means of discreet suggestion the more emphatic and experimental metrical forms of the sixteenth century to suggest complexities of feeling not possible in those metrical forms as the poets of the sixteenth century used them. He suggests the song-books in his devotional poetry, as he therein utilizes the common imagery of the Petrarchan love lyric. Dr. W. C. Williams, an experimental poet by virtue of his meter, is in other qualities of his language one of the most richly traditional poets of the past hundred and fifty years; in fact, making allowances for his somewhat narrow intellectual scope, one would be tempted to compare him, in this respect, to such poets as Hardy and Bridges. No two experimental conventions will have similar poetic results; one cannot predicate a great deal that is important of experimental poetry in general; but, as one might suspect, some forms of experimental poetry have had dire results, and of individual types of convention one can frequently say a great deal.

73

III. *Pseudo-traditional or "literary" poetry* is the work of writers insufficiently aware of what they have stylistically and morally in common with the best poetry of the race to master this common element (I am referring, of course, to a common distinction, skill, and moral intelligence, that which one may find in Campion, Jonson, and Herrick) and in a manner of speaking to take it for granted. The literary poet, cut off from his tradition by education, for he usually occurs in the late eighteenth, the nineteenth, or the twentieth century, regards the tradition as something exotic, and employs it accordingly. He imitates the idioms of the traditional poet, but they are no longer for him familiar and exact; they are foreign and decorative; they degenerate into mannerism. He comes to regard certain words, phrases, or rhythms, as intrinsically poetic, rather than as instruments of perception or as the clues to generative ideas. His imitation is thus crude, as we can see by comparing the pseudo-Elizabethan meters of Beddoes to the meters of Campion, the meters of Chatterton to the meters of the best lyrics of the thirteenth century, the meters of Swinburne to the meters of Sidney, from which they are frequently derived.

When, as in the traditional poet, the wisdom and expression of the past are both a basic part of the individual, when they are at once taken casually for granted and thoroughly understood, the individual contribution to the poem can be made with force and precision. But if the combiner of two elements understands only one of them, the combination will hardly be satisfactory; and in this instance it is unlikely that the comprehension of only one element is possible: it is both or nothing. A purely literary poet can very likely never exist; the literary quality rather invades the work in a greater or smaller measure. Swinburne is one of the best examples which I know of a poet of a fairly high order of talent whose work is pretty evenly corrupted by "literary" habits. Mr. T. S. Eliot's essay on Swinburne defines the quality admirably. Symons, Wilde, and Dowson carry farther what Swinburne began: their poetry is almost devoid of meaning.

74

As one approaches a norm, one's variations from that norm take on more significance. If the convention of a poem is badly defined, the poetry is vague. This is one of the many things wrong with most of Shelley, Byron, Hugo, De Musset, Lamartine, and the other typical romantics. The same weakness inheres in some measure in Swinburne, though Swinburne's vagueness is commonly of a more consistent quality.

The "literary," of course, is what commonly appears traditional to the popular and even the academic taste: Swinburne is preferred to Landor, and Housman to Bridges. The traditional is ordinarily thrust aside as merely literary; or else, in such poets as Crashaw or Williams, it is completely overlooked because the reader is nonplussed by experimental elements. We have nothing but Arnold's touchstones to guide us in this difficulty, and our own hard work to make us worthy of guidance; that, and the Grace of God. It is an obscure procedure, but Landor is surely greater than Swinburne and Bridges than Housman.

IV. *Pseudo-experimental poetry* is the work of a poet who confuses tradition with convention, and who, desiring to experiment, sees no way to escape from or alter tradition save by the abandonment of convention: it means the abandonment of form and of poetry. Mr. E. E. Cummings is a good example of this type of poet. When Mr. Cummings ceases to experiment, and essays the traditional, he becomes painfully literary. Either way he shows little comprehension of poetry.

To what extent can the principles herein defined, be brought to the defense of the methods employed by the experimental poets of twentieth century America and of the French Symbolist School, methods to which I have elsewhere objected? Any answer must be prefaced with the warning that what is true of one type of convention need not be true of another. What is true even of one sub-type need not be true of another sub-type of the same group: consider, for example, the number and variety of the forms of pseudo-reference.

The convention of heightened intensity is sound procedure in Williams' poem *On the road to the contagious hospital,* which I have discussed at length, because there is poetic justification, a genuine motivation, for the conventional language, and the conventional language is graduated to the wholly poetic with great skill and energy. Were there no such justification, however, the poem would belong, with many of H. D.'s poems on Greek landscape, in the class of implicit reference to a non-existent symbolic value. Much of Wordworth's more or less Miltonic grandiloquence belongs in the same class: the grandeur never emerges or emerges too seldom. Bryant is sometimes similar, when he applies a tone of moral grandeur to material that is purely physical and unable to support such a tone.

The pseudo-reference of T. S. Eliot's *Gerontion,* partly a matter of reference to non-existent plots, partly a matter of purely grammatical logic, seems in some ways to resemble the heightened intensity employed by Dr. Williams in *On the road to the contagious hospital.* That is, while Dr. Williams, in certain passages, assumes more feeling than he perceives, Mr. Eliot, in certain passages, assumes more reasonableness than he perceives. Dr. Williams works up to passages in which his claims are supported by perception; so does Mr. Eliot; and in each poem these passages represent the core of the poem, not only as regards feeling, but as regards rational theme. The climax of Mr. Eliot's poem, the passage beginning: "I that was near your heart was removed therefrom," justly one of the most famous passages in recent poetry, is probably greater than anything in the poem by Dr. Williams, though perhaps not so much greater as Mr. Eliot's admirers (who commonly fail to understand Dr. Williams altogether) might be ready to believe.

On the other hand, Dr. Williams' poem is far more solidly written. The fine passages in *Gerontion,* though frequently of a

76

magnificent precision in themselves, arise from a mass of carefully veiled imprecisions, which, on first glance, appear to have more meaning than they really have. The success of conventional language of this kind depends very largely on the reader's being more or less deluded: the procedure in Dr. Williams' poem is at once more in the open and more definite, and one knows what is happening at every instant. There are moments in Mr. Eliot's poem at which no one can be really sure of what is going on, and as a result one feels, or I cannot escape feeling, a degree of uncertainty in the very essence of the poem. One has again, perhaps, the fallacy of imitative form: the attempt to express a state of uncertainty by uncertainty of expression; whereas the sound procedure would be to make a lucid and controlled statement regarding the condition of uncertainty, a procedure, however, which would require that the poet understand the nature of uncertainty, not that he be uncertain. *Gerontion,* at any rate, is the most skillful modern poem in English to employ any large measure of pseudo-reference; the superiority of its pseudo-reference to most of that of Crane and of Yeats probably derives from the fact that it is deliberate, whereas theirs is commonly in a large part unintentional—in *Gerontion* it is mystification instead of confusion, or at least is employed willfully and deliberately as a means of bringing certain recognized, and, for the author, irreducible confusion, under a little control.

To cite another example of pseudo-reference, Hart Crane's poem *The Dance* reverses the order of conventional and poetic language employed by Williams. That is, Williams' language is largely conventional in the early part of the poem, and then takes on poetic fullness at the climax. Crane's poem, on the other hand, displays most of its fully poetic content (the purely but brilliantly descriptive writing) scattered through the first half, approximately, of the poem, and then breaks into a complete disjunction of feeling and meaning at the climax.

The purely grammatical logic of much of *Faustus and Helen,* parts I and III, might be in a measure defensible on the same grounds as the pseudo-reference of *Gerontion,* or to the same extent, except that there is a much greater proportion of pseudo-reference in the poem by Crane and that there is much less clarity as to the general theme, so that the moments of coherence are never sufficient to give any perceptible support to the conglomeration of conventional language.

But we may probably say for any kind of pseudo-reference that it goes through the forms of reasonable statement and hence may be a preparation for reasonable statement, or a stop-gap between passages of reasonable statement, and that, if it does not occur in great excess and is distributed in small enough bits, if, in short, it is not too obtrusive and is not too seriously involved in the very conception of the poem, it may do relatively little harm and so be accepted at times as an apparently inevitable evil.

Laforguian irony, however, is not a preparation for anything else, is not an unfulfilled form, but is merely a slipshod attitude, final in itself, and invariably a vice of feeling. Qualitative progression, likewise, is not a preparation for anything else; it offers no unfulfilled claims or half-utilized machinery. If it is central to the structure of the work—that is, if the theme is really unformulable and merely a mood—it is a vice for the reasons which I have given elsewhere. It is legitimate only when used occasionally and in an impure way, as Mr. Burke has shown it in use on the periphery of *Hamlet.*

We may say in general, then, that some kinds of experimental convention are more dangerous than others, and the more recent types appear to be the most dangerous, perhaps because they have been used more boldly—or rather, more rashly—than experimental conventions have ever been used before. Secondly and finally, traditional poetry is the most economically and firmly constructed variety possible. To see this, one has only to compare Bridges' *The southwind strengthens to a gale* to *Gerontion* or to *The Dance.*

PRIMITIVISM AND DECADENCE

THE dichotomy of major and minor poetry is obviously unsatisfactory, nor is the reason for this the one so often given, that general descriptive terms have no meaning. They can at least be given meaning. If Ben Jonson is a major poet and Campion a minor poet, it is patently outrageous to apply either epithet to Byron; yet Byron for the present has a place in our literature, and, though it seems incredible that he should be read as long as Jonson or as Campion, it is probable that he will be read for a long time. Of Jonson and Campion we may say that both are masters; few men have lived to write as well; it is unlikely that many men have lived to appreciate them fully. Their difference is mainly a difference of scope; the achievement of Campion cannot be dimmed by comparison with the achievement of the greatest poets, for within its scope it is unimpeachable. The achievement of Byron, or the other hand, suffers by comparison with the work of any of the minor masters, even with that of Googe or Turberville; in a superficial sense he attempted as much as did Jonson, but he understood with precision nothing that he touched, and his art he understood least of all.

The more important poets might be placed in four groups: the second-rate, those whose gift for language is inadequate to their task, poets such as Byron, D. H. Lawrence, or Poe, and regardless of their other virtues or failings; the major, those who possess all of the virtues, both of form and of range; the primitive, those who utilize all of the means necessary to the most vigorous form, but whose range of material is limited; and the decadent, those who display a fine sensitivity to language and who may have a very wide scope, but whose work is incomplete formally (in the manner of the pseudo-referent and qualitative poets) or is somewhat but not too seriously weakened by a vice of feeling (in the manner of the better post-romantic ironists). The second type of decadent poets may differ from the second-rate only in degree of weakness. In this essay I shall endeavor to discover some of the implications of the terms *decadent* and *primitive* as used in this way. The nature of major poetry and of the second-rate should be reasonably obvious, even though there might be disagreement over examples.

It will be seen that most experimental poetry, particularly experimental poetry of the types developed in the late nineteenth and early twentieth centuries, appears to issue either in primitivism or in decadence, if it issues in nothing worse. The term *primitivism,* however, may be allowed to include traditional minor poetry as well.

If we compare *The Dance,* by Hart Crane, to one of the better poems of Jonson or of George Herbert, it is decadent in the sense in which I have just defined the term: it is incomplete poetry. Historically, however, Crane's poetry is related not only to Jonson, but to the romantics, especially to Whitman, much of whose doctrine Crane adopts. Whitman's doctrine is illusory: like all of the anti-rational doctrines of the past two centuries, it vanishes if pursued by definition. Whitman, as a second-rate poet, however, was equipped to write of it, after a fashion, without rendering its nature immediately evident. His poetic language was as vague as his expository; he had no capacity for any feeling save of the cloudiest and most general kind. Crane's poetic gift is finer than Whitman's, and the precision of his language forces one to recognize the inadequacy of his reference. If he is decadent in comparison to Jonson, he yet marks an advance in relationship to Whitman. It would probably be easier to convince most readers at present that something is wrong with Crane than that something is wrong with Whitman. The reason for this is simple: one observes rather quickly that something is wrong with Crane, because something is right, and one is thus able to get one's bearings. From one point of view his language is frequently that of a

80

master. Nowhere in Whitman can one find such splendor or even such precision of language as in *The Dance* or as in *The River*. And if one proceeds from these to his most finished performances, *Repose of Rivers, Faustus and Helen II,* and *Voyages II,* one has poems in which the trace of decadence is scarcely discernible.[1] It would not have been impossible, then, for Crane to decrease the amount of pseudo-reference in his poems; as a decadent poet, he was not bound to deteriorate; nor does his poetry indicate that contemporary literature is in a state of·deterioration.

Mr. Pound's *Cantos* are decadent in relation to *Paradise Lost,* since their structure is purely qualitative. But, historically, there is probably another relationship to Whitman here, in which Mr.

---

[1] Of *Repose of Rivers* one may say that the individual images are miraculous, but that their order is not invariably necessary; this fact, combined with the lack of rhythmical conviction as the poet proceeds from one image to the next, results in a frail, almost tentative structure. *Faustus and Helen II* is purely descriptive and hence offers no temptations to sin; the fantastic subject matter, combined with the relative safety of the approach, enabled Crane to utilize his entire talent for rhetorical ingenuity without risk of its betraying him. In *Voyages II,* which seems to me his greatest poem, he disciplined this talent to meet a more dangerous and exacting theme, and achieved greater solidity than in *Repose of Rivers.*

It will be observed that my selections do not coincide with those of Mr. Allen Tate. Mr. Tate speaks of *The River* as Crane's "most complex and sustained performance, a masterpiece of æsthetic form," and of *Praise for an Urn* as "the finest elegy in American poetry" (Hound and Horn: Summer, 1932). This seems to me sheer nonsense. The latter poem is metrically a very stiff and inexpert free verse; except for the two striking lines about the clock and half a dozen other passable lines, it is sentimental and affected. "The slant moon on the slanting hill," "Delicate riders of the storm," "The everlasting eyes of Pierrot/ and of Gargantua the laughter," are sentimental clichés of the twenties, and their quality pervades the whole poem. As to *The River,* it is as ineptly put together as any romantic poem I have read: the poem should begin with the passage about the cannery works, and everything previous should be discarded; about half the lines from the cannery works to the Pullman breakfasters should be revised, the eyeless fish, the old gods of the rain, and much of the rest of it being the shoddiest of decoration, not even skillful charlatanry; and in the last part of the poem, which is the finest and which is very powerful, there are still bad lines, for examples, "Throb past the city storied of three thrones," "All fades but one thin skyline 'round. . . . Ahead," and the two final lines of the poem: The defects of *The River* are not due to the theme, but merely to carelessness, and could easily have been revised away. The pantheism which wrecks *The Dance* appears in *The River* in a fairly harmless form, and merely lends pathos to certain lines, particularly to those describing the end of **Dan Midland.**

81

Pound shows not decay but growth. It is not a relationship of theme, as in Crane's poetry, but one of form. Mr. Pound's long line is in part a refinement of Whitman's line; his progression from image to image resembles Whitman's in everything save Whitman's lack of skill. The *Cantos* are structurally Whitmanian songs, dealing with non-Whitmanian matter, and displaying at their best great suavity and beauty. As Crane shifts out of pseudo-reference into rational reference in *Voyages II,* so Mr. Pound in his versions of Propertius, using the same form as in the *Cantos,* produces coherent comment on formulable themes, or does so part of the time. The change may be due to the genius of Propertius, but it is possible in Mr. Pound's form. The form, however, would not permit of any very rapid or compact reasoning.

I have elsewhere suggested that post-romantic irony represents an advance over the uncritical emotionalism of such poets as Hugo or Shelley, in so far as it represents the first step in a diagnosis.

The primitive poet is the major poet on a smaller scale. The decadent poet is the major, or primitive, poet with some important faculty absent from the texture of all his work. Dr. Williams is a good example of the type of poet whom I should call the contemporary primitive. His best poems display no trace of the formal inadequacies which I have mentioned as the signs of decadence. Such poems as *The Widow's Lament* or *To Waken an Old Lady* are fully realized; the form is complete and perfect; the feeling is sound. Dr. Williams has a surer feeling for language than any other poet of his generation, save, perhaps, Stevens at his best. But he is wholly incapable of coherent thought and he had not the good fortune to receive a coherent system as his birthright. His expository writing is largely incomprehensible; his novel, *A Voyage to Pagany,* displays an almost ludicrous inability to motivate a long narrative. His experience is disconnected and fragmentary, but sometimes a fragment is wrought to great beauty. His widest range has been reached in a

82

single piece of prose, *The Destruction of Tenochtitlan,* in which he found his material more or less ready for treatment in the form of history: in treating it, he achieved one of the few great prose styles of our time.[1]

Dr. Williams bears a certain resemblance to the best lyric poets of the thirteenth century: there is in both an extreme sophistication of style, a naïve limitation of theme (Dr. Williams has a wider range than the early poets, however) and a fresh enthusiasm for the theme. It was out of such poetry as *Alisoun* that English poetry little by little grew. Sidney represents a resurgence of the same quality at a later date, but touched with Petrarchan decadence.[2] Decadent poetry, as I have defined it, would have been impossible in thirteenth century England: it requires a mature poetry as a background.

A decadent poet such as Crane may, as I have said, if considered historically, represent a gain and not a loss. As a matter of fact, he may embody the most economical method of recovery for an old and rich tradition in a state of collapse, for he offers all of the machinery of a mature and complicated poetry. Both decadent and primitive lack an understanding and correlation of their experience: the primitive accepts his limitations through wisdom or ignorance; the decadent endeavors to conceal them, or, like some primitives, may never discover them; the primitive, however, treats of what he understands and the decadent of more than he understands. For either to achieve major poetry there is necessary an intellectual clarification of some kind. But to attain

---

[1] In connection with the fragmentariness, the primitivism, of this piece, it is worth noting that the rhetoric, perhaps merely because of the perfection to which it raises traditional heroic prose, resembles closely that of Macaulay's *History,* the passage in Macaulay describing the formation and character of Cromwell's army, offering especially striking similarity. Macaulay *chose* to write a five volume work, one of the supreme English masterpieces, in this style. Dr. Williams *happened* to write a twelve-page masterpiece in the style, or so one is forced to conclude from the quality of most of his prose.

[2] In connection with this statement and others regarding the lyrics of the sixteenth century, see my review of the *Oxford Book of 16th Century Verse,* edited by E. K. Chambers, in the Hound and Horn, Volume VI, Number 4.

major poetry from the position of a primitive poet such as Dr. Williams might necessitate the creation of a good deal of technical machinery as well; whereas the pseudo-referent poet has most of his machinery made and already partly in action.

There is probably the same relationship between the Petrarchan rhetoric of the sixteenth century, with its decorative and more or less pseudo-referent conceit, and the best Metaphysical verse of the seventeenth century. In Shakespeare's sonnets the rhetoric is Petrarchan, yet the Petrarchan conceit is given a weight of meaning new to it; something similar occurs in the poetry of Fulke Greville. The gap between the sonnets of Shakespeare and the sonnets of Donne is not extremely great. Yet the best thirteenth century lyrics, like the best early Tudor lyrics, those by such men as Vaux, Googe, Gascoigne, and Turberville, are better poetry than the work of Daniel or of Drayton, in spite of the fact that they would have been less immediately useful in certain ways to Donne. So with our contemporaries: Dr. Williams is more consistently excellent than Crane, and at his best is possibly better. Crane's machinery, convenient as it might at any moment prove, remains, so long as it is not utilized, a source of confusion.

The decadent poetry of Mr. Pound does not appear to me to provide so many opportunities for filling out as does that of Crane, partly because of the meter, which presents a problem too elaborate in itself for discussion here, and partly because all, or nearly all, superfluous machinery in the way of pseudo-referent forms has been avoided. That is, the difficulty of extending the usefulness of a convention may often bear a direct relationship to the perfection with which the convention accomplishes the aims for which it was created.

A perfect primitive poet is not of necessity better than a decadent poet, though he may be; in fact a decadent poet may seem of greater value than a poet whom one might call major. Some major poets are greater than others, and a poem by Mr. Stevens, technically decadent because tinged with his vice—*Of the Manner*

84

of *Addressing Clouds,* for example—may suffer extremely little from its decadence and be in other respects a poem of tremendous power.

The poetry of Mr. Paul Valéry demonstrates that decadence may be a very economical mode of recovery. Mr. Valéry was formed in the influence of the Symbolists, poets decadent, frequently, in the same way as the Americans of the second and third decades of the twentieth century. The poet who illustrates this point more clearly than any other in English is Mr. T. Sturge Moore, who shares in a considerable measure the background of Mr. Valéry.

Mr. J. V. Cunningham, in the Commonweal for July 27, 1932, describes Mr. Moore's favorite theme as that "spiritual pride which would overreach natural limits . . . the effort to violate human relationships by imposing one's identity on others," together with criticism of such spiritual pride. Mr. Cunningham cites the excellent poem *On Four Poplars* as an instance of the subject matter, and other poems could be cited. The theme, however, is not limited to the ethical sphere in Mr. Moore, but has its religious counterpart, in a mysticism related to that of poets so diverse as Hart Crane and Robinson Jeffers, which leads to the attempt to violate our relationship with God, or with whatever myth we put in his place, even with Nothingness, and which leads concurrently to the minimizing of moral distinctions, that is, of the careful perception of strictly human experience. Mr. Moore differs from the Romantic mystics in defining this temptation without succumbing; in defining not only the temptation but its legitimate uses, and its dangers. His repeated poems on the subject of Silence, and his repeated references to Semele, are among the more obvious indications of his interest in the subject. His great lyric *To Silence* may be taken as an allegorical summary of this theme and of his own relationship to romantic tradition, the tradition of rejuvenation through immersion in pure feeling, or sensation, the immersion which is the mystical communion of the romantic, and which occurs in its most perfect literary examples among the devotees of imitative form to be found in the French Symbolist and American Experimental schools.

Mr. Moore's immersion has actually led to rejuvenation, to an inexhaustibly fascinating freshness of perception: the immersion of other poets has too often led to disintegration. I quote the entire text of the poem *To Silence:*

> *O deep and clear as is the sky,*
> *A soul is as a bird in thee*
> *That travels on and on; so I,*
> *Like a snared linnet, now break free,*
> *Who sought thee once with leisured grace*
> *As hale youth seeks the sea's warm bays.*
>
> *And as a floating nereid sleeps*
> *In the deep-billowed ocean-stream;*
> *And by some goat-herd on lone rock*
> *Is thought a corpse, though she may dream*
> *And profit by both health and ease*
> *Nursed on those high green rolling seas,—*
>
> *Long once I drifted in thy tide,*
> *Appearing dead to those I passed;*
> *Yet lived in thee, and dreamed, and waked*
> *Twice what I had been. Now, I cast*
> *Me broken on thy buoyant deep*
> *And dreamless in thy calm would sleep.*
>
> *Silence, I almost now believe*
> *Thou art the speech on lips divine,*
> *Their greatest kindness to their child.*
> *Yet I, who for all wisdom pine,*
> *Seek thee but as a bather swims*
> *To refresh and not dissolve his limbs:—*

Though these be thine, who asked and had,
And asked and had again, again,
Yet always found they wanted more
Till craving grew to be a pain;
And they at last to silence fled,
Glad to lose all for which they pled.

O pure and wide as is the sky,
Heal me, yet give me back to life!
Though thou foresee the day when I,
Sated with failure, dead to strife,
Shall seek in thee my being's end,
Still be to my fond hope a friend.

The structure of the poem is logical and the reference is exact, but the feeling is very strange. There is a remarkable freshness of sensitivity, yet it is a different freshness from that of a primitive, such as Dr. Williams. It might almost be characterized as the hypersensitivity of convalescence: the poet is minutely sensitive to dangers and meanings past but imminent, to which Dr. Williams is not only insensitive but of the very existence of which he is unaware.

If we can imagine that human experience is portrayable geometrically as a continuous circle on which there are equally spaced points, A, C, E, and G, and that classical poetry has been written with these as its chief points of reference, we can then imagine a breakdown, a period of confusion, in which these points are lost, but after which a new set of points, B, D, F, and H, also spaced equally but not the same points, are established. These new points would give a comparable balance, or intelligence, perhaps, but an altered view of the detail, that is, an altered quality of perception, of feeling. Or it might be that the old points would merely be regained after the breakdown, the quality of the perception being then affected by the past experience of the breakdown.

It is as if we extended the allegory of the poem just quoted, thus: Silence is equal to pure quality, unclassified sensation (a purely hypothetical infinity, which, however, we can approach indefinitely),[1] and the immersion in sensation (or confusion) amounts to the dissolution of one's previous standards in order to obtain a fresh sensibility. This is what the romantic movement amounted to, the degree of dissolution varying with each poet, regardless of whether the dissolution was necessary. Mr. Moore states explicitly, however, in this poem and in others, not only the value of the immersion, but its peril, and the need of the return. This does not mean that Mr. Moore at any point in his career has performed experiments like those of Rimbaud or of Joyce; he has not done so publicly, and there is no reason to suppose that he has done so privately. But his sensibility was profoundly affected by those who did perform them; he is a part of the tradition that had at an earlier point in its history subjected itself to the immersion; his private history as a poet begins at the point in the history of the tradition at which recovery has begun, and his talents enable him to bring that recovery to its highest pitch of development; but he remembers and understands what preceded him, and his sensibility bears witness to the fact. He thus resembles Paul Valéry, though of the two poets his relationship to the Symbolist tradition is perhaps the more obvious. The feeling of strangeness and freshness is still upon Mr. Moore's

---

[1] Cf. Morris Cohen, *Reason and Nature,* page 37: "Avenarius wishes to purify our world-view by returning to the natural view of experience as it existed before it was vitiated by the sophistications of thought (in the form of introjection). But the empiricist's uncritical use of the category of the *given,* and the nominalistic dogma that relations are created rather than discovered by thought, lead Avenarius to banish not only animism and other myths, but also the categories, substance, causality, etc., as inventions of the mind. In doing this he runs afoul of the great insight of Kant that without concepts or catergories percepts are blind." Also Allen Tate, *The Fallacy of Humanism,* in *The Critique of Humanism* (Brewer and Warren: 1930): "Pure Quality is nature itself because it is the source of experience. . . . Pure Quality would be pure evil, and it is only through the means of our recovery from a lasting immersion in it . . . that any man survives the present hour; pure Quality is pure disintegration."

poetry, as upon one who has just emerged from the sea. One should examine in particular the following poems: *To Silence, To Slow Music, From Titian's Bacchanal,* the first half of the double sonnet *Silence, Love's First Communion, An Aged Beauty's Prayer, The Deeper Desire,* the sonnets on Sappho, *Semele, Io, Suggested by the Representation on a Grecian Amphora, The Song of Chiron, Tragic Fates, To a Child Listening to a Repeater,* and, among his longer works, *Daimonassa* (perhaps his greatest single achievement), *Marianne, The Sea Is Kind, The Centaur's Booty,* and *The Rout of the Amazons.*

The term *decadence* is frequently used to denote or connote personal immorality, yet even in this sense the historical defense is sometimes effective. There is no doubt that Verlaine was personally childish, sentimental, and debauched. He was in some ways one of the most muddled souls of a muddled century: his life was pseudo-referent even though his poetry was frequently not, and, like his poetry, was too often governed wholly by mood. He was not, as Baudelaire was, morally intelligent among whatever sins he may have committed, and was never much the wiser for his sins or wrote better poetry because of them. The greater part of his life was simply confusion; yet a narrow margin of it he evaluated with precision; to that extent he was superior to such formless predecessors as Lamartine or de Musset, who smeared everything with a consistent texture of falsity. As a poet, Verlaine at his best was rather a primitive than a decadent, for his poetry is not ambitious; his best art was as natural and proper, if we consider his situation in time and space, and potentially as valuable to his successors, as was the art of the author of *Alisoun.*

I do not mean that Verlaine's limitations were inevitable, however. In offering an historical excuse for decadence, formal or personal, I do not mean to imply that there is ever an historical necessity for either, but merely that life is painful if one expects more than two or three men in a century to behave as rational animals, and that for a good many men there are mitigating cir-

89

cumstances. Baudelaire ran through romanticism early in his career, to achieve the most remarkable balance of powers in French literature after Racine; he had no need of several generations of graduated decadence; his recovery was accomplished at a bound. He was determined by his period only to this extent: that he dealt with the problem of evil in the terms in which he had met it, the terms of the romantic view of life; and it was because of these terms that he was able to embody the universal principles of evil in the experience of his own age and evaluate that experience.

Our own position may be similar. If we doubt the value of the romantic communion, if we cannot see that the poet who has survived it is a better poet for it, we may at least say this: that the communion, as we have experienced it historically, if not personally, has extended our knowledge of evil and so made us wiser; for the moral intelligence is merely the knowledge and evaluation of evil; and the moral intelligence is the measure of the man and of the poet alike. It may seem a hard thing to say of that troubled and magnificent spirit, Hart Crane, that we shall remember him chiefly for his having shown us a new mode of damnation, yet it is for this that we remember Orestes, and Crane has in addition the glory of being, if not his own Æschylus, perhaps, in some fragmentary manner, his own Euripides.

Again, we should remember that there is no certitude that several generations of graduated decadence will lead to recovery; they may lead merely to a general condition of hypochondria. Crane's first book was better than his second, and the work of his last few years displays utter collapse. T. S. Eliot abandoned Laforguian irony not to correct his feelings, but to remain satisfied with them: his career since has been largely a career of what one might call psychic impressionism, a formless curiosity concerning queer feelings which are related to odds and ends of more or less profound thought. There is current at present a very general opinion that it is impossible in our time to write good poetry in

90

the mode, let us say, of Bridges, either because of the kind of poetry that has been written since ("the stylistic advances of Eliot and of Pound"), or because of social conditions ("the chaos of modern thought"), or because of both, or because of something else. I believe this to be a form of group hypochondria. The simple fact of the matter is, that it is harder to imitate Bridges than to imitate Pound or Eliot, as it is harder to appreciate him, because Bridges is a finer poet and a saner man; he knows more than they, and to meet him on his own ground we must know more than to meet them.

Many experimental poets, by limiting themselves to an abnormal convention, limit themselves in range or in approach: that is, become primitives or decadents of necessity; and they lack the energy or ability to break free of the elaborate and mechanical habits which they have, in perfecting, imposed upon themselves. Miss Moore, Dr. Williams, Gerard Hopkins, and Ezra Pound might all serve as examples. In other words, the selection of a convention is a very serious matter; and the poet who sets out to widen his tradition may often succeed only in narrowing or sterilizing himself. Crashaw's experimenting at its wildest gets wholly out of hand and becomes pseudo-referent decadence. Nevertheless, the experimenting of Donne and of Crashaw is subject to the check of a comprehensible philosophy, as the experimentalism of Pound and of Crane is not. The experimentalism of Milton was subject to such a check and was, I think one may say, necessitated by the unprecedented scope of his plan and by the unprecedented violence and magnificence of his mind, but this is not to say that he was the greatest of poets, though he was, of course, one of the greatest.

The relationship between experimentalism, decadence, and primitivism is thus seen to be intimate, though it would be rash to formulate many laws of the relationship.

Decadent poetry may be valuable as a point of departure, either to its authors or to others, exactly in so far as its deficiencies are

91

recognized and are susceptible of correction. Not all types of decadent poetry need be equally valuable in this respect, though the understanding of one may equal in value the understanding of another as a form of moral knowledge. Unless the deficiencies of a decadent convention are recognized, there is little likelihood that the convention will be improved; there is great likelihood that it will deteriorate; for it is the nature of man to deteriorate unless he recognizes the tendency and the source of the deterioration and expends actual effort to reduce them.

THE INFLUENCE OF METER ON POETIC CONVENTION

SECTION I: FOREWORD

I HAVE endeavored to show in other essays that the morality of poetry is inextricably involved in its form, and in a particular essay that it is closely related to the *convention,* or norm of feeling, of any particular poem, and to certain general types of convention. As the norm of a poem will set certain limits upon the range and procedure and quality of feeling possible within the poem, we may say that a convention, whether we take the term in the specific or in the generic sense, has a life of its own to which the poet is largely subjected once he has adopted it. I have tried to indicate, in discussing the idea of convention, that meter plays an important part in the establishment of convention. I shall now endeavor to draw certain general conclusions regarding the poetic effectiveness of a few basic types of meter.

This essay will be divided into five sections, as follows:

The first section comprises the present descriptive foreword.

The second section contains a brief sketch of the theory of traditional English meter on which my scansion of experimental meter and my theories regarding the relationship of meter to poetic convention are based.

The third section is a study of the scansion of free verse and of the influence of free verse rhythms upon poetic convention. I have begun this analysis with specimens of my own free verse because I can speak of my own intentions with a certain amount of authority. I have proceeded thence to the poets from whose practice I derived my own. I am not sure, however, that my own poems offer the clearest illustrations available with which to introduce the medium to the reader unfamiliar with its principles. The

93

deliberate effort which I made in most of these poems to introduce a substructure, iambic as to beat, but not pentameter, as a
kind of counterpoint to the free-verse beat, probably renders
much of my free-verse too difficult for the beginner to scan and
may even ruin much of it entirely. The specimens from Dr.
Williams, H. D., and Mr. Wallace Stevens, however, though they
possess great finish and variety of movement, probably keep the
metrical norm a little more obviously in view. If the reader finds
the meter of my own poems obscure, therefore, he might fairly
reserve his incredulity regarding the system of scansion until
after he shall have studied the specimens of scansion from the
other writers.

Even so, I have little hope that many readers will understand
the scansion that I propose for free verse, chiefly because an understanding of it requires a very thorough knowledge of all the
best poems employing the medium in the second and third decades of our century, a sensitive and conscientious study of several
years in duration, the immersion of the student in a particular
way of feeling, the acquisition of a new and difficult set of habits
of hearing and of audible reading. This discipline is arduous
and on the face of it is not particularly tempting: there are so
many other things that one can do instead. In the few years past,
the discipline has been almost wholly abandoned save by the few
poets of the Experimental Generation [1] whose sensibilities were
largely formed in this discipline. The most distinguished poets
of the Reactionary Generation [1] who have attempted free verse—

---

[1] For the sake of a few loose but usable terms, I offer the following classification of 20th century poetry in English: I. The Generation of Forerunners:
Hardy, Bridges, Yeats, T. Sturge Moore, and Alice Meynell; II. The Generation
of Transition: Robinson, Frost, and Agnes Lee; III. The Experimental Generation: Stevens, Williams, Miss Moore, Miss Loy, Joyce (whose prose is related in
important ways to the verse of his contemporaries), Adelaide Carpsey, Pound,
Eliot, H. D., and Lawrence; IV. The Reactionary Generation: Crane (a member
of this group, instead of the last, solely by virtue of his dates, personal affiliations,
and inability to write or understand free verse), Tate, Baker, Blackmur, Clayton
Stafford, Louise Bogan, Grant Code, J. V. Cunningham, Don Stanford, Barbara
Gibbs. Mr. J. C. Ransom is a kind of ambiguous and unhappy though sometimes

Hart Crane and Louise Bogan, for example—have been wholly unsuccessful in their brief and rare excursions into the medium. The Experimental poets who mastered the medium, it is worth observing, were those who for some years were more or less fanatical on the subject and gave themselves over to it wholly or almost wholly: Wallace Stevens is perhaps the only poet living who has practiced the new and the old meters simultaneously and at a high level of excellence. Very few readers, even professionally literary and academic readers, will give the subject the attention necessary for even a preliminary perception of it, but I am certain of the soundness of my scansion and wish to set it on record, for it will be of value to students here and there as time goes on.

For the present, suffice it to say that my *objections* to free verse do not depend upon the scansion of free verse, whether the verse be mine or that of any other; the objections are more cogent if the verse cannot be scanned. My system of scansion is offered by way of a preliminary defense of the medium, to show what it really has accomplished, and to limit as far as possible my objections, which, in my opinion, have only a narrow, though a quite definite, margin of relevancy. The objections are closely related to objections which I have made elsewhere to the other aspects of the recent experimental conventions.

The fourth section will deal with the relationship of experimental to traditional meters, the examples being drawn mainly from the sixteenth and seventeenth centuries, and will endeavor to show that the relationships are more fruitful of good within the old framework of accentual-syllabic meters than within, or in connection with, the framework of free verse.

---

distinguished connective between this group and the last. The direction and significance of this group are clearest in Howard Baker, in a little of Tate, and in the writing, very small in bulk at present, of Stafford, Stanford, Cunningham, and perhaps Miss Gibbs. Such a classification omits good poets here and there: de la Mare and Viola Meynell cannot quite be included; the most important omission is Elizabeth Daryush, the finest British poet since T. Sturge Moore.

The fifth section will give a brief summary of the history and principles of the heroic couplet, and of its effect upon poetic convention in the past, and a brief comparison of the powers of the heroic couplet (one of the most thoroughly traditional of all forms) with the powers of the forms that have been used in recent years to take something resembling its place: Websterian verse, the long free-verse line, stemming from Whitman and brought to its greatest perfection by Pound and by Miss Moore, and the syllabic meters of Robert Bridges.

Although this essay does not cover every known form of meter, it should be kept in mind that it does cover the following fields: the chief types of modern experimental meter in their relationship to convention (that is, the common varieties of lyrical free verse, and of semi-didactic free verse, Websterian verse, and the accentual and syllabic systems of Hopkins and of Bridges), the principles of traditional meter in its relationship to convention, and the principles of the relationships between traditional and experimental meters. That, as nearly as I can discover, is the entire bearing of the subject of meter on my present studies.

SECTION II: GENERAL PRINCIPLES OF METER

The poetic line, as I understand the subject, has at one time or another been constructed according to four different systems of measurement: the quantitative, or classical system, according to which a given type of line has a given number of feet, the feet being of certain recognized types and being constructed on the basis of the lengths of the component syllables; the accentual, or Anglo-Saxon, system, according to which the line possesses a certain number of accents, the remainder of the line not being measured, a system of which free verse is a recent and especially complex subdivision; the syllabic, or French, system, according to which a line is measured solely by the number of syllables which it contains; and the accentual-syllabic, or English, system, which

96

in reality is identical with the classical system in its most general principles, except that accented and unaccented syllables displace long and short as the basis of constructing the foot, and that pyrrhic and spondaic feet seldom occur and might in fact be regarded as ideally impossible because of the way in which accent is determined, a matter which I shall presently discuss.

Mechanically perfect meter, were it possible, would be lifeless; meter of which the variation is purely accidental is, like all other manifestations of pure accident, awkward and without character. There are in English accentual syllabic meter the following principles of variation, if no others:

(1) *Substitution:* That is, an inverted or trisyllabic or other foot may be substituted for an iambic foot in an iambic line, or similar alterations may be introduced into other lines. The method of substitution varies with writers and with periods. In the blank verse of Ben Jonson, there is a taut regularity, the result of the very careful manipulation of iambic and trochaic feet; and then occasionally there occurs a trisyllabic substitution, which effects a nervous leap, as suddenly stilled as it was undertaken:

> *Thou vermin, have I ta'en thee out of dung,*
> *So poor, so wretched, when no living thing*
> *Would keep thee company but a spider or worse?*

The device of trisyllabic and even of quatrosyllabic substitution is practiced by Webster to such an extent that the verse norm almost disappears, and certain passages are interpreted by some editors as prose and by others as verse, with about an equal show of reason. Milton, on the other hand, is extremely cautious in the use of trisyllabic feet—his extra syllables are all but lost in elision —but he goes very far in the use of trochaic feet and of trochaic words in iambic feet. To illustrate the use of the trochaic word in the iambic foot, we may employ the first line of Jonson's lyric, *Drink to me only with thine eyes.* Here we have a trochee for the first foot and iambs for the remainder; but the word *only* is

97

itself trochaic and echoes the trochaic foot with which the line opens and at the same time functions in two iambic feet.

(2) *Quantity*. Quantity is an element of poetic rhythm in every language, regardless of whether the measure is based upon it. In French, a relatively unaccented language of which the verse is purely syllabic, quantity and phrase-stress, which are governed by no set rules, provide the chief sources of variation; in English, quantity provides one major source of variation.

In an iambic foot, for example, the unaccented syllable may be short and the accented syllable long (there is no strict dividing point, of course, between short and long, no two syllables being of identical length, and no arbitrary categories being necessary where the measure is not based upon quantity): such a foot will seem to be very heavily marked. On the other hand, it is quite possible for the unaccented syllable to be very long and the accented syllable very short—consider, for example, the first foot, a strictly iambic one, in this line of *The Nightingales,* by Robert Bridges:

Nay, barren are those mountains and spent the streams.

The variations resulting from this principle can be very finely shaded; so much so, in fact, as to obscure the accent on some occasions.

(3) *Varying Degress of Accent.* Accent, like quantity, is unlimited in its variations. In practice, the manner of distinguishing between an accented and an unaccented syllable is superior, I believe, to the manner of distinguishing in classical verse between a long syllable and a short. In English verse, a syllable is accented or unaccented wholly in relation to the other syllables in the same foot, whereas in classical verse each syllable is arbitrarily classified by rule, and its length is in a very small measure dependent upon the context. This makes for a greater fluidity and sensitivity in English, I suspect, and with no loss of precision, perhaps with a gain in precision. It also renders the spondaic and pyrrhic feet

98

theoretically impossible, as I have said, though they may sometimes be approximated; a close approximation of a pyrrhic is usually followed by a close approximation of a spondaic as in the following line:

Through rest or motion the noon walks the same.[1]

The latter half of the word *motion* and the article following form a fair pyrrhic, the two subsequent words a spondaic.

If we take Ben Jonson's line, "Drink to me only with thine eyes," we find that *with* is accented in relation to the syllable preceding it, but that it is more lightly accented than the unaccented syllable of the subsequent foot. One has, in other words, a mounting series of four accents, which can be formally divided into two iambic feet, and which is in addition emphasized by an almost equally progressive quantitative series. A very slight shift of emphasis in each of these two feet would have made them resemble the two in the line previously quoted, the pyrrhic followed by the spondaic; yet the pyrrhic-spondaic combination appears strikingly abnormal as one reads it, and the sequence by Jonson glides by almost imperceptibly.

This rule in regard to the variation of accent is normally overlooked by metrists; it is wholly overlooked, for example, by Robert Bridges. The oversight results in Bridges' refusal to differentiate, so far as terminology is concerned—though he differentiates sharply in actual practice—between what I have called accentual-syllabic and syllabic meters: Bridges applies the term syllabic indiscriminately to both, and this confusion vitiates in a serious manner, I believe, the general conclusions of his work on Milton's prosody: he scans Milton incorrectly, it appears to me, for this reason, and more particularly Milton's later work, which merely represents learned variation to an extreme degree from a perfectly perceptible accentual-syllabic norm, variation expressive of very violent feeling.

---

[1] From *Noon at Neebish*, by Don Stanford, Hound and Horn VII-4.

(4) *Sprung Meter.* Sprung meter is loosely described by Hopkins in his preface to his poems. It consists essentially of the juxtaposition of heavily and more or less equally accented syllables by other means than normal metrical inversion; it is thus a normal and characteristic phenomenon of English syllabic meter, as written by Robert Bridges and by Elizabeth Daryush, meter in which accents may be combined at will, since they have no part in the measure, and it is equally characteristic of purely accentual meter, in which the measure is based on the number of accents and on nothing else, so that monosyllabic feet may easily occur in sequence. When sprung meter occurs as a variant of normal accentual-syllabic meter, it represents, actually, the abandonment, for the moment, of the accentual-syllabic norm in favor either of the syllabic or of an accentual norm.

Wyatt employs the accentual variety of sprung rhythm, that in which an unaccented syllable is dropped from between two accented, so that a monosyllabic foot occurs, as in the second line below:

> *They flee from me, that sometimes did me seek*
> *With naked foot, stalking in my chamber.*[1]

Robert Green, whom Hopkins names as the last English poet to use sprung meter, employs the same species as a variant on his seven-syllable-couplets:

> *Up I start, forth went I,*
> *With her face to feed mine eye.*[2]

The norm of this line is iambic tetrameter, with the initial unaccented syllable omitted; in the first line above, an additional unaccented syllable is dropped between the second and third accented. Green often writes a line of this kind, but with the initial unaccented syllable returned to its place, so that the syllable count is undisturbed:

---

[1] and [2] *Oxford Book of 16th Century Verse,* pages 51, 382, and 381.

100

> *That when I woke, I 'gan swear,*
> *Phyllis' beauty palm did bear.*[1]

A more normal, perhaps a more true, example of syllabic sprung rhythm within an accentual syllable poem, is the following line from a poem by Barnabe Googe, *Of Money:*[2]

> *Fair face show friends when riches do abound.*

Here the accentual weight of the first and third places is increased to equal approximately the weight of the second and fourth; we might describe the first two feet as spondaic, except that, as there is no compensatory pair of pyrrhics, two extra accents are introduced into the line, with the result that the accentual measure is abandoned and we have no measure left save the purely syllabic.

Robert Bridges' poem, *A Passerby,* whatever may have been the intention of the author, can be scanned as a poem in iambic meter, pentameter and hexameter, with certain normal substitutions, and with examples at irregular intervals of both kinds of sprung meter.

The first of the two lines below, written by the present author, contains both kinds of sprung meter within a single line:

> *Warm mind, warm heart, beam, bolt, and lock,*
> *You hold the love you took, and now at length. . . .*[3]

The first four syllables are modeled on the first four in the line by Googe; the next two shift to accentual meter, for each represents a single foot; the last two syllables are a perfect iambic foot. The line is a variant within a sonnet in iambic pentameter; it contains, according to the scansion just given, eight syllables, five feet, seven accented syllables (six of them being in unbroken sequence), and one unaccented syllable. Variants so extraordinary

---

[1] *Oxford Book of 16th Century Verse,* pages 51, 382, and 381.

[2] Arber's English Reprints.

[3] In a pamphlet called *Before Disaster,* published by Tryon Pamphlets, Tryon, N. C.

101

as this are seldom wholly admirable, and this one is offered primarily as an example and a curiosity.

The reader will find a particularly fine example of sprung meter in a poem wholly syllabic, in *Still-Life,* by Elizabeth Daryush;[1] of sprung meter in a poem wholly accentual in *The Windhover,* by Gerard Hopkins.

SECTION III: THE SCANSION OF FREE VERSE

I shall begin the description of my system for the scansion of free verse with an account of two poems of my own and of what I endeavored to accomplish in them. The foot which I have used consists of one heavily accented syllable, an unlimited number of unaccented syllables, and an unlimited number of syllables of secondary accent. This resembles the accentual meter of Hopkins, except that Hopkins employed rhyme. He appears to have had the secondary accent, or subordinate and extra-metrical "foot," in mind, when he spoke of "hangers" and "outrides."

Accents, as I have already pointed out, cannot be placed in a definite number of arbitrary categories; language is fluid, and a syllable is accented in a certain way only in relation to the rest of the foot. The secondary accent is discernible as a type if the poet makes it so. A dozen types of accent are possible in theory, but in practice no more than two can be kept distinct in the mind; in fact it is not always easy to keep two.

Ambiguity of accent will be more common in such verse as I am describing than in the older verse, but up to a certain point this is not a defect, this kind of ambiguity being one of the chief beauties of Milton's verse, for example. The poet must be permit-

---

[1] This poem appears in full near the end of this book, and is quoted from *The Last Man, and Other Poems,* by Elizabeth Daryush, Oxford Press, England. Mrs. Daryush has published four other books of importance: Verses: First to Fourth Books inclusive. She is one of the few great poets living, and is all but unknown.

ted to use his judgment in dubious instances, and the critic must do his best to perceive the reason for any decision. Quantity will obviously complicate this type of foot more than it will the foot of the more familiar meters.

I shall mark and discuss two poems of my own, and shall then proceed to specimens of free verse from some of the chief poets of the Experimental generation, upon whose work my own ear for this medium was trained. Since a line which is complete metrically may for the sake of emphasis be printed as two lines, I shall place a cross-bar (/) at the end of each complete line. I shall number the lines which are so marked, for ease in reference. Lines which are incomplete metrically, but which are independent and not parts of complete lines, will likewise be marked and numbered, and these lines will also be marked with an asterisk (*). I shall mark each primary stress with double points (″) and each secondary stress with a single point (′).

"Quod Tegit Omnia"

1. *Earth dărḳens and is b̈eaded/*
2. *with a swéat of b̈ushes ánd/*
3. *the b̈ear comes fórth:*
   the mínd stored with/
4. *magníficénce procëeds intó/*
5. *the mýsterý of Tíme, nów/*
6. *c̈ertain óf its chöice of/*
7. *p̈assion but úncértain óf the/*
8. *p̈assion's ën̈d.*

When/

9. *Pláto témporízes on the nä̈ture/*
10. *of the plümage óf the söul, the/*
11. *wïnd hums ín the f̈eathers ás/*
12. *acróss a c̈órd impëccable ín/*
13. *täutness but of nö mínd:/*

103

           the sine-póndere, móst/
15   impertürbable of ëlemènts,/
16   assümes its öwn propörtions/
17   silently, of its öwn pröperties—/
18   an ëxcellénce at whïch óne
           sïghs./

19   Advënturer in
           living fáct, the póet/
20   móunts intó the sprïng/
21   upón his töngue the täste of/
22   aïr becóming bódy: ïs/
23   Embëdded in thïs crÿstallïne/
24   precïpitáte of Tïme./

There are no incomplete lines in the preceding poem, though a few lines are broken in two for the sake of emphasis.

The next poem is more difficult. I shall mark it as if it contained two feet to the line, and as if most of the lines were printed in two parts. The imperfect lines (unassimilable half-lines) are marked with a single asterisk (*). Unbroken lines are marked with a double asterisk (**).

The Bitter Moon

1   Dry snöw runs búrning
        on the gröund like fïre—/
2   the quíck of Héll spin ón
        the wind. Should Í belíeve/
3   in thïs your bódy, táke it
        at its wörd? I háve belíeved/
4   in nóthing. Eärth burns with a
        shádow thát has héld my/
5   flésh; the ëye is a shádow
        that consümes the mínd/

6   * Scréam into äir! The vóices/
7   ** Of the déad still víbrate—/
8   théy will fínd them, thréading
       áll the pást with twínging/
9   ** wíres alíve like häir in cóld./
10   * Thése are the nérves/
11 ** of déath. Í am its bräin./

12 ** Yóu are the wäy, the oäth/
13   I táke. I hóld to thís—
       I bént and thwárted by a wíll/
14 ** to líve amóng the líving déad/
15 ** instéad of the dead líving; Í/
16   * becóme a vóice to sóund for./
17 ** Can you féel through Spáce,/
18 ** imägine beyond Tíme?
                          The/
19   snów alive with möonlight
       lícks abóut my änkles./
20 ** Can you fínd this énd?/

This poem is marked, as I have said, as if it contained two feet
to the line. It is possible, however, to regard the poem as having
a one-foot line, in which case the lines marked with the single
asterisk and those unmarked are regular, and those marked with
the double asterisk are irregular. The two-foot hypothesis involves
the smaller number of irregular lines, and it would eliminate for
this poem a difficulty in the matter of theory; to wit the question of whether a one-foot line is a practical possibility. Consider,
for example, the possibility of a poem in iambic lines of one foot
each. The poem will be, if unrhymed, equaled to an indefinite
progression of iambic prose. But in reply, one may object that
except for iambic pentameter, and except for occasional imitations
of classical verse, no unrhymed verse has ever been successful in
English in the past, and that Herrick, at any rate, composed one

excellent poem in lines each of one iambic foot ("Thus I / Pass by / To Die," etc.) I believe that this discussion will show that the secondary accent makes possible the use of unrhymed lines of any length, from one foot up to as many as can be managed in any other form of meter whether rhymed or not.

In the poem preceding the last, there was very little difficulty in distinguishing between the primary and the secondary accents; the trouble lay in distinguishing between secondary accents and unaccented syllables. But when, as here, it is the two types of stress that are hard to separate, we stand in danger of losing entirely our system of measurement. Now, if the meter is success-ful, there are in this poem two meters running concurrently and providing a kind of counterpoint: one is the free-verse meter, marked by the heavy beats, and the other is an iambic meter, marked by all the beats, whether heavy or light. The poem can-not be arranged in blank verse, however, for the iambic passages are incomplete, are fragments laid in here and there to provide musical complication and for the sake of their connotative value. If the heavy beats cannot be heard as distinct from the light, then the free verse scheme vanishes and one has left only a frag-mentary blank verse, badly arranged.

Mr. William Rose Benét, in the Saturday Review of Literature (New York) for September 6, 1930, objected to the structure of my own free verse, at the same time offering realignments of two passages, which he regarded as superior to my own alignments. A few weeks later, he published a letter from myself, which stated, and for the first time in public, the general principles which I am now discussing. One of his revisions was of the open-ing lines of the poem which I have just quoted. He heard only the incomplete blank verse and rearranged the passage accord-ingly, some of the available fragments of blank verse, however, being broken in ways that were to myself inexplicable.

My own free verse was very often balanced on this particular tight-rope. During the period in which I was composing it, I was

106

much interested in the possibility of making the stanza and wherever possible the poem a single rhythmic unit, of which the line was a part not sharply separate. This effect I endeavored to achieve by the use of run-over lines, a device I took over from Dr. Williams, Miss Moore, and Hopkins, and by the extreme use of a continuous iambic undercurrent, so arranged that it could not be written successfully as blank verse and that it would smooth over the gap from one line of free verse to the next.

In the standard meters, the run-over line tends to be awkward because of the heavy rhythmic pause at the end of each line: Milton alone, perhaps, has been highly and uniformly successful in the employment of the device, and he has been so by virtue of the greatest example of the grand manner in literature, a convention so heightened as to enable him to employ this device, which in most poets is destructively violent, as a basis for sensitive modulations of rhetoric. Even in Websterian verse the line-end is too heavily marked for the run-over to be pleasing. But if the *rhythm* can be made to run on rapidly, the meaning can be allowed to do so with impunity: hence the terminations in articles, adjectives, and similar words so common in free verse of this type, and even the frequent terminations in mid-word to be observed in Hopkins and in Miss Moore, this last liberty, of course, being common also in classical verse, in which, as in much free verse, the line-end pause is frequently extremely slight. Of the dangers of this type of free verse I shall have more to say later.

In the poem last quoted, much of the metrical ambiguity arises from the use of an unusually long foot, which allows quantity an opportunity somewhat greater than usual to obscure the accent. In the line, "at its word? I have believed," *word* receives the primary accent, but *believed,* which receives a secondary accent, is longer and may seem more heavily accented to the unwary. In the line "flesh; the eye is a shadow," the heavy accent goes to *eye,* but *flesh,* because of its position at the beginning of the line and before the semi-colon, receives more length than it would receive in most other places, and may seem for the moment to receive the main accent. In most cases, the reader will find that the ambiguity is one of alternatives; that is, he will naturally place a heavy accent on one word or on the other, so that the pattern will not be damaged. Ambiguities of this sort, and within the limits just mentioned, may be a source of value; they are, as I have said, one of the principle beauties of Milton's versification. If the ambiguity, in free verse, however, ceases to be a hesitation between alternatives, and becomes more general, the metrical norm is destroyed.

The poets from whom I learned to write free verse are probably better subjects than myself for a demonstration of the theory. The poem quoted below, which is by Dr. Williams, contains two lines of double length, each of which I have marked with an asterisk:

To Waken an Old Lady

1	Old äge is
2	a flíght of smäll
3	cheéping bïrds
4	skïmming
5	bare trëes
6	abóve a snöw glaze.
7	* Gäining and fäiling,
8	théy are büffeted
9	by a därk wind—
10	but whät?
11	Ón the härsh wëedstalks
12	the flöck has résted—
13	the snöw
14	is cövered with bróken
15	sëed-husks,

16   *and the wind témpered*
17   *with a shríll*
18   * *píping of plénty.*

It will be observed that free verse requires a good deal of variation from line to line if the poem is to keep moving, and that as the one-foot line permits only a limited amount of variation if the foot is not to be stretched out to the danger-point, the poet must choose between a very short poem and a good sprinkling of irregular lines.

H. D.'s *Orchard* is one of the principal masterpieces of the free-verse movement. It employs a one-foot line, with fourteen lines of double length out of a total of thirty lines:

1   *I sáw the first péar*
2   *As it féll.*
3   * *The hóney-séeking, gólden-bánded,*
4   *The yéllow swárm*
5   *Was nót more fléet than Í*
6   * *(Spáre us fróm lóvelinéss!)*
7   *And I féll próstrate,*
8   *Crýing*
9   * *"Yóu have fláyed us with your blóssoms;*
10   * *Spáre us the béauty*
11   *Of frúit-trees!"*

12   *The hóney-séeking*
13   *Páused not;*
14   * *The áir thúndered their sóng*
15   * *And Í alóne was próstrate.*

16   *O róugh-héwn*
17   *Gód of the órchard*
18   * *I bríng yóu an óffering;*
19   *Do yóu alóne unbéautiful*

109

20   *Són of the gód*

21   * *Spáre us fróm lóveliness!*

22   *These fállen házel-núts*

23   * *Stripped láte of their gréen shéaths;*

24   * *Grápes, red-púrple,*

25   *Their bérries*

26   * *Drípping with wíne;*

27   * *Pómegránates alréady bróken*

28   *And shrúnken fígs*

29   * *And quínces untóuched*

30   * *I bríng you as óffering.*

Some of the details of this poem should be mentioned. Where there is a long foot, the heavily accented syllable usually appears to receive much less weight than in a short foot, the crowd of minor syllables absorbing emphasis from the major syllable. This absorption is sometimes, though not invariably, facilitated by the placing of two long feet in a single line. Line three is an example of this rule; line nine is an exception to it. The position of the accent in these lines is relevant to their respective effects: in line three, the accent is at the beginning of each foot, with the secondary accent and the unaccented syllables following in a rapid flicker, an arrangement which makes for speed; in line nine, the accent falls near the end of the foot, an arrangement which makes for a heavy stop; in both lines the second foot repeats the arrangement of the first foot, except for the very light syllable before the first heavy accent in line three, an arrangement which makes for clarity and emphasis of rhythm.

If the reader will examine again some of the preceding poems, he will find that this device of occasional repetition, either within the line or from line to line, may be used effectively for another purpose: it may provide the poet with a kind of pause, or moment of balance, between different movements, both of them

110

rapid, a pause which is roughly analogous to a pause at the end of a line in the older meters.

Miss Marianne Moore has carried the method of continuity, of unbroken rush, farther than anyone, not even excepting Hopkins. The following lines are from her poem, *A Grave*. Since an extremely long foot is employed, in an extremely long line, I have placed a cross-bar at the end of each foot:

1   *mén lower néts,/ unconscious óf the fáct/ that théy are désecráting/ a gráve,/*
2   *and row quíckly/ awáy/ the bládes/ of the öars/*
3   *möving togéther líke the/ féet of wáter-spiders/as íf there wére no such thíng/ as déath./*
4   *The wrínkles progréss/ upón themsélves in a phálanx,/ beáutiful/ únder nétworks of fóam,/*
5   *and fáde bréathlesslý/ while the séa rústles/in and öut of/ the séaweed./*

Most of the generalizations drawn from the poem by H. D. could be as well illustrated by examples taken from this passage.

I have spoken of the remarkably continuous movement in Miss Moore's verse; but Miss Moore is seldom wholly at one with her meter. There may be, as in this passage, brilliant onomotopoetic effects, but the breathlessness of the movement is usually in contrast to the minuteness of the details, and this contrast frequently strengthens the half-ominous, half-ironic quality of the details, at the same time that it is drawing them rather forcibly into a single pattern. This is not a defect, at least in the shorter poems: it is a means of saying something that could have been said in no other way; and what is said is valuable. But the instrument is highly specialized and has a very narrow range of effectiveness.

A further danger inherent in the instrument becomes apparent in Miss Moore's longer poems, such as *Marriage* and *The Octopus*. These poems are at once satiric and didactic, but the statiric and didactic forms require of their very nature a coherent ra-

111

tional frame. The poems have no such frame, but are essentially fragmentary and disconnected. The meter, however, is emphatically continuous, and creates a kind of temporary illusion of complete continuity: it is a conventional continuity which never receives its justification. Despite the brilliance of much of the detail, this unsupported convention is as disappointing as the Miltonic convention in Thomson; it is a meaningless shell. In the shorter poems, the stated theme often correlates the details raitonally.

Dr. W. C. Williams once remarked to me in a letter that free verse was to him a means of obtaining widely varying speeds within a given type of foot. I believe that this describes what we have seen taking place in the examples of free verse which I have analyzed. But if the secondary accent becomes negligible for many lines in sequence, if, in other words, the speed from foot to foot does not vary widely, the poem becomes one of two things: if the accentuation is regular, the poem is unrhymed metrical verse of the old sort; or if the accentuation is irregular, the poem may be a loose unrhymed doggerel but will probably be prose. Or there may be an uneven mixture of regularity and of irregularity, which is the possibility least to be desired.

The opening of Richard Aldington's *Choricos* illustrates the mixture of free and regular verse:

1 *The ancient songs*
2 *Pass deathward mournfully.*

3 *Cold lips that sing no more, and withered wreaths,*
4 *Regretful eyes, and drooping breasts and wings—*
5 *Symbols of ancient songs*
6 *Mournfully passing*
7 *Down to the great white surges. . . .*

The first four lines comprise three perfect lines of blank verse.

112

Elsewhere in the same poem, we may find free verse abandoned for prose, the line-endings serving only as a kind of punctuation:

1   *And silently,*
2   *And with slow feet approaching,*
3   *And with bowed head and unlit eyes*
4   *We kneel before thee,*
5   *And thou, leaning toward us,*
6   *Caressingly layest upon us*
7   *Flowers from thy thin cold hands;*
8   *And, smiling as a chaste woman*
9   *Knowing love in her heart,*
10   *Thou sealest our eyes.*
11   *And the illimitable quietude*
12   *Comes gently upon us.*

The first three lines of this passage might pass for free verse of the same kind that Mr. Aldington has used elsewhere in the same poem, but line four, in spite of the fact that it can be given two major accents, does not continue the movement previously established. Line eight is similarly troublesome, and the remaining lines are uncertain. The difficulty is not mathematical but rhythmic: the movement of the lines in the context is awkward and breaks down the context.

This passage raises and answers a rather troublesome question. It is possible that any passage of prose—even the prose that I am now writing—might be marked off into more or less discernible feet of the kind that I have described, each foot having a heavy accent and one or more or perhaps no light accents, and a varying number of relatively unaccented syllables. These feet could then be written one or two or three to a line. Would the result be free verse? I believe not.

We are supposing in the first place that the writer of prose will instinctively choose syllables that fall naturally into three clearly discernible classes; whereas this classification of syllables in free verse is, in the long run, the result of a deliberate choice, even though the poet may be guided only by ear and not by theory. But let us for the sake of argument neglect this objection.

The accented syllables are necessary to free verse, but more is necessary: the remaining syllables must be disposed in such a way as to establish an harmonious and continuous movement. But can the laws of this harmonious and continuous movement be defined? That is, can one define every possible type of free verse foot and can one then establish all of the combinations possible and rule out all the unsatisfactory combinations? I have never gone into this subject experimentally, but I believe that one can demonstrate rationally that the compilation of such laws is impossible.

The free verse foot is very long, or is likely to be. No two feet composed of different words can ever have exactly the same values either of accent or of quantity. If one will mark off the passage quoted from Mr. Aldington, for example, one will get certain combinations which are unsuccessful; but one cannot say that the duplication of the same series of accent marks in a different group of words will be unsuccessful, because the duplication of accent marks will not mean the duplication of the exact weights and lengths of the original passage. The free verse foot is simply too long and too complicated to be handled in this way. If the reader feels that this proves free verse to be no verse at all, I have two answers: first, that he will have the same difficulty with any other purely accentual verse, from the Anglo-Saxon to Hopkins and with any purely syllabic; secondly, that if the rhythms which I have described can be *perceived* in a fairly large number of poems, and if the failure to establish such rhythms can be perceived in other poems, one has a rhythmic system distinguishable from prose and frequently of poetic intensity, and it matters very little what name it goes by. What is really important is the extent of its usefulness, its effect upon poetic convention.

114

I do not wish to claim that the poets of whom I write in this essay had my system of scansion in mind when writing their poems. Probably none of them had it. What I wish to claim is this: that the really good free verse of the movement can be scanned in this way, and that the nature of our language and the difficulties of abandoning the old forms led inevitably to this system, though frequently by way of a good deal of uncertain experimenting.

Mr. Aldington's *Choricos* is an attempt to combine certain traditional meters, English and classical, and a little biblical prose, in a single poem, just as Hugo, for example, employed different meters in a single poem, but this procedure, whether employed by Hugo or by Richard Aldington, is inevitably too loose to be satisfactory. Other poets have quite deliberately employed simple prose rhythms. Sometimes the prose is very good, as in *One City Only,* by Alice Corbin, or as in a few poems by Mina Loy. But it is not verse, and it is not often a satisfactory medium for poetic writing.

The masters of free verse of the Experimental Generation are William Carlos Williams, Ezra Pound, Marianne Moore, Wallace Stevens, H. D., and perhaps Mina Loy in a few poems, though the movement of Mina Loy's verse is usually so simplified, so denuded of secondary accent, as to be indistinguishable from prose. Mr. Eliot never got beyond Websterian verse, a bastard variety, though in *Gerontion,* he handled it with great skill—with far greater skill than Webster usually expends upon it. Mr. T. Sturge Moore, at the very beginning of the twentieth century, published a very brilliant and very curious specimen of experimental meter, in *The Rout of the Amazons,* which, like the neo-Websterian verse of Mr. Eliot and of others, employs blank verse as its norm, but departs farther from the norm than the neo-Websterian poets have been able to depart, and, unlike the neo-Websterian verse, never seems to approach prose, but rather approaches a firm and controlled free verse as its extreme limit.

115

Free verse has been all but abandoned by the next generation: a few good specimens are to be found in minor poems by Glenway Wescott, Grant Code, and the late Kathleen Tankersley Young; but Messrs. Wescott and Code have written their best poems in other forms, and so have all of their ablest contemporaries.

A major objection to free verse as it has been written by H. D., Dr. Williams, and perhaps others, and the objection can be raised against much of Hopkins as well, is this: that it tends to a rapid run-over line, so that the poem, or in the case of a fairly long poem, the stanza or paragraph, is likely to be the most important rhythmic unit, the lines being secondary. Hopkins was aware of this tendency in his poems, but apparently not of its danger. In his own preface to his poems, he writes: ". . . it is natural . . . for the lines to be *rove over,* that is, for the scanning of each line immediately to take up that of the one before, so that if the first has one or more syllables at its end the other must have as many the less at its beginning; and in fact the scanning runs on without break from the beginning, say, of a stanza to the end and all the stanza is one long strain, though written in lines asunder." The result is a kind of breathless rush, which may very well be exciting, but which tends to exclude or to falsify all save a certain kind of feeling, by enforcing what I have called, in my essay on Poetic Convention, a convention of heightened intensity.

Hopkins meets the difficulty by excluding from his poetry nearly all feeling that is not ecstatic; Dr. Williams meets it by allowing and utilizing a great deal of language that is largely conventional. But if a poem is written wholly in conventional language, it becomes, when the convention is of this type, merely melodramatic and violent, and, when the convention is of some other type, weak in some other and corresponding manner. Dr. Williams has thrown away much good material thus; so has H. D. done; and so have others.

The extremely abnormal convention is seldom necessary, I be-

116

lieve, to the expression of powerful feeling. Shakespeare can be just as mad in a sonnet as can Hopkins, and he can be at the same time a great many other things which Hopkins cannot be. He has a more limber medium and is able to deal with more complex feelings. I mean by this, that if no one quality receives extreme emphasis, many diverse qualities may be controlled simultaneously, but that if one single quality (the ecstasy of the thirteenth century lyric, *Alisoun,* for example) does receive extreme emphasis, it crowds other qualities out of the poem. The meter, the entire tone, of *Alisoun,* render impossible the overtone of grief which would have been present had Hardy dealt with the same material, and which would have given the poem greater scope, greater universality. One may state it as a general law, moral as well as metrical, that an increase in complexity commonly results in a decrease in emphasis: extreme emphasis, with the resultant limitation of scope, is a form of unbalance. Sexual experience is over-emphasized in the works of D. H. Lawrence, because Lawrence understood so little else—and consequently understood sexual experience so ill. In a very few poems, notably in the sonnet *To R. B.,* Hopkins avoids his usual tone in a considerable measure, by reverting toward standard meter. His rhymes and his consequent independence of the secondary accent enable him to do this, but a similar reversion is impossible in free verse, a medium in which the reversion would simply result in a break-down of form. It is difficult to achieve in free verse the freedom of movement and the range of material offered one by the older forms.

A few poems appear to indicate that a greater variety of feeling is possible in free verse, however, than one might be led to suspect by the poems thus far quoted. One of the best is *The Snow Man,* by Wallace Stevens:

1   * One must háve a mínd of wínter
2   To regãrd the frõst and the bõughs
3   Of the píne-trees crústed with snõw;

4   And háve been cóld a lŏng tíme
5 * Tó behŏld the jŭnipérs shăgged with ĭce,
6   The sprúces rŏugh in the dĭstant glĭtter

7   Óf the Jánuáry sŭn; and nŏt to thĭnk
8   Of ány mísery in the sŏund of the wĭnd,
9   In the sŏund of a fĕw léaves,

10 * Which is the sŏund of the lănd
11   Fúll of the sáme wĭnd
12   That is blŏwing in the sáme báre pláce

13   For the lístenér, who lĭstens in the snŏw,
14   And, nŏthing himsélf, behŏlds
15 * Nŏthing thát is nŏt thére and the nŏthing that ĭs.

The norm is of three beats, and there are four irregular lines, the first and third having two beats each, the second and fourth having four. Each line in this poem ends on a very heavy pause, provides, that is, a long moment of balance before the next movement begins. The manner in which the secondary accents are disposed in the fifth, sixth, and seventh lines, in order to level and accelerate the line, is remarkably fine, as is also the manner in which the beat becomes slow and heavy in the next few lines and the way in which the two movements are resolved at the close. There is complete repose between the lines, great speed and great slowness within the line, and all in a very short poem. Dr. Williams has got comparable effects here and there. The following poem by Dr. Williams is called *The Widow's Lament in Springtime:*

1   Sórrow ís my ŏwn yárd
2   Whére the nĕw gráss
3   Flámes as ĭt has flámed
4   óften befŏre, but nŏt
5   with the cŏld fĭre

6   that clóses róund me thís yéar.

7   Thírty-fíve yéars

8   I líved with mý húsband.

9   The plúm-tree ís whíte todáy

10   with másses of flówers.

11   Másses of flówers

12   lóad the chérry bránches

13   and cólor sóme búshes

14   yéllow ánd sóme réd,

15   but the gríef in my héart

16   is strónger than théy;

17   for thóugh they wére my jóy

18   fórmerlý, todáy I nótice thém

19   and túrn awáy forgétting.

20   Todáy my són tóld me

21   * Thát in the méadow

22   at the édge of the héavy wóods

23   in the dístance, he sáw

24   trées of whíte flówers.

25   I féel that Í would líke

26   * to gó there

27   and fáll into those flówers

28   * and sínk into the mársh néar them.

The slow heavy movement of this poem of two-foot lines is accentuated by the periodic swift lines (four, six, nine, thirteen and fourteen, seventeen and eighteen and nineteen, twenty-two, along with a few more or less intermediate lines, like one, ten, eleven, twelve, and twenty-eight) out of which the slow lines fall with greater emphasis. A poem of much greater length which displays a remarkable range of feeling is Mr. T. Sturge Moore's play (or, to be more exact, Eclogue) entitled *The Rout of the Amazons*. Mr. Pound's *Cantos* offer a slow and deliberative movement, but are as bound to it as is H. D. to her ecstasy.

There are at least two additional objections which I should mention in connection with the tyranny of free-verse movements, objections perhaps inclusive or causative of those already made; namely, that two of the principles of variation—substitution and immeasurably variable degrees of accent—which are open to the poet employing the old meters, are not open to the poet employing free verse, for, as regards substitution, there is no normal foot from which to depart, and, as regards accent, there is no foot to indicate which syllables are to be considered accented, but the accented syllable must identify itself in relation to the entire line, the result being that accents are of fairly fixed degrees, and certain ranges of possible accent are necessarily represented by gaps. In free verse the only norm, so far as the structure of the foot is concerned, is perpetual variation, and the only principle governing the selection of any foot is a feeling of rhythmical continuity; and on the other hand the norm of the line, a certain number of accents of recognizably constant intensity, and in spite of the presence of the relatively variable secondary accents, inevitably results in the species of inflexibility which we have seen equally in the fast meters of Williams and in the slow meters of Pound.

The free-verse poet, however, achieves effects roughly comparable to those of substitution in the old meters in two ways: first by the use of lines of irregular length, a device which he employs much more commonly than does the poet of the old meters and with an effect quite foreign to the effect of too few or of extra feet in the old meters; and, secondly, since the norm is perpetual variation, by the approximate repetition of a foot or of a series of feet. It is a question whether such effects can be employed with a subtlety equal to that of fine substitution. Personally I am convinced that they cannot be; for in traditional verse, each variation, no matter how slight, is exactly perceptible and as a result can be given exact meaning as an act of moral perception. Exactness of language is always a great advantage,

120

and the deficiencies of free verse in this respect will be more evident after an examination of some of the traditional meters.

SECTION IV: EXPERIMENTAL AND TRADITIONAL METERS

In describing the consequences of the swifter forms of free verse and of the meters of Hopkins, I have indicated a general principle which accounts for a definite and often-regretted tendency in the history of English meter—the tendency of successive generations of poets to level their meters more and more toward the iambic, that is, toward the normal meter of the language, and at the same time to simplify their rhyme schemes, to depart, at least, from those schemes, which, like that of *Alisoun,* contribute to a swift and lilting music or to some other highly specialized effect. Without assuming the truth of any theories of evolution, of progress, or of continuous development in poetry, we may recognize the facts that within limited historical patterns, early poetry is simple and later poetry is likely to be relatively complex, these two adjectives being understood as relating to the content of the poetry, the moral consciousness of the art; that, as the complex poetry deadens, or, the commoner phenomenon, as the critical sensibility to it deadens and the fashion begins to change, there are likely to be new outbreaks of emphatic and relatively simple, but nevertheless fresh, feeling, which eventually may reinvigorate the older tradition.

How, then, can one reconcile in theory this tendency to increasing complexity of feeling with the tendency to increasing simplicity of means? The answer, I believe, is fairly simple. The nearer a norm a writer hovers, the more able is he to vary his feelings in opposite or even in many directions, and the more significant will be his variations. I have observed elsewhere that variations of any kind are more important in proportion as they are habitually less pronounced: a man who speaks habitually at the top of his voice cannot raise his voice, but a man who speaks

121

quietly commands attention by means of a minute inflection. So elaborately and emphatically joyous a poem as *Alisoun*, for example, can be only and exclusively joyous; but Hardy, in the more level and calmer song, *During Wind and Rain*, can define a joy fully as profound, indeed more profound, at the same time that he is dealing primarily with a tragic theme. To extend the comparison to free verse, H. D.'s *Orchard* is purely ecstatic; it is as limited in its theme as is *Alisoun*, and as specialized in its meter. But Dr. Williams' poem, *The Widow's Lament*, is at once simpler and calmer in meter and more profound in feeling. The difference between these two poems, of course, is due wholly to a difference in temperament, and not to the passage of centuries. That a specimen of free verse can be found displaying a complexity and a profundity comparable to those of such poems as Hardy's *During Wind and Rain* and Bridges' *Love not too much*, I do not believe; nor do I believe that such a poem can ever be composed. For reasons that will become increasingly clear as this discussion progresses, I believe that the nature of free verse is a permanent obstacle to such a composition.

It is worth noting that the songs of Shakespeare are, for the most part, the most varied and brilliant exhibitions of minutely skillful writing which we possess, as well as the most song-like of songs. They are likewise nearly as frail, nearly as minor, as any wholly successful poetry could be. The sonnets, on the other hand, remain, I suppose, our standard of the greatest possible poetry; they are written in the normal line of our poetry and in the simplest form of the sonnet.

The lilting movement of the sixteenth century lyrical meters, of Sidney, of *England's Helicon*, disappears from the work of the great masters of the seventeenth century. Even Herrick suggests the old feeling ever so slightly, though quite deliberately—his line has a stony solidity utterly foreign to the lyrics of fifty years earlier. Donne employs at times movements which suggest the earlier movements, as, for example, in the songs, *Sweetest love I*

122

do not go, and *Go and catch a falling star,* but his bony step is wholly different from the light pausing and shifting of Sidney; it is a grimly serious parody. George Herbert's *Church Monuments,* perhaps the most polished and urbane poem of the Metaphysical School and one of the half dozen most profound, is written in an iambic pentameter line so carefully modulated, and with its rhymes so carefully concealed at different and unexpected points in the syntax, that the poem suggests something of the quiet plainness of excellent prose without losing the organization and variety of verse.

Crashaw, in his most beautiful devotional poetry, employs cadences and imagery suggestive of earlier love poetry and drinking songs. Thus, in his paraphrase of the *Twenty-third Psalm,* he writes:

> *When my wayward breath is flying,*
> *He calls home my soul from dying.*

This passage corresponds closely to a passage in a translation made by Crashaw from an Italian love song, a fact which might lead one to suspect that he sought deliberately for relationships between disparate modes of experience and that the correspondences—and there are many of them—in his other poems are not accidental:

> *When my dying*
> *Life is flying,*
> *Those sweet airs, that often slew me*
> *Shall revive me,*
> *Or reprieve me,*
> *And to many deaths renew me.*

The reader should observe that there is here not only a resemblance between the first couplet of the translated stanza and the couplet of the psalm, but that the traditional image of physical love, as it appears in the translated stanza, serves as a basis for the image of salvation in the psalm; something similar occurs at the climax of the famous poem to Saint Theresa; similar also is the use, in his various references to the Virgin, of imagery borrowed from Petrarchan love-poetry; similar also is his application of Petrarchan wit to sacred subjects, as if he were, like some celestial tumbler, displaying his finest training and ingenuity for the greater glory, and out of the purest love, of God—in fact, it is in Crashaw that the relationship between the Petrarchan conceit and the Metaphysical conceit is perhaps most obvious. The paraphrase of the psalm, which is the more complex and profound of the two poems just mentioned, is written in couplets and exhibits very few feminine rhymes. The sudden shift into the feminine rhyme in this particular couplet gives an unexpected and swiftly dissipated feeling of an earlier, more emphatic, and more naïve lyricism.

In the following couplet, likewise from the paraphrase of the psalm, there is both in the meter and in the imagery a strong suggestion of the poetry of conviviality:

> *How my head in ointment swims!*
> *How my cup o'erlooks her brims!*

The head, of course, is not swimming with drink, and the cup is the cup of bliss, but the instant of delirium is deliberately sought and impeccably fixed. The meter contributes to this effect in two ways: through the approximate coincidence of length and accent, with the resultant swift and simplified movement, and through the almost exact metrical similarity of the two lines. The spiritualization, if one may employ such a term, of the convivial image is partly, of course, the work of the context, but it is also, in a large measure, the work of the startling word *o'erlooks,* which takes the place of the commoner and purely physical *o'erflows:* the word not only implies animation, but suggests a trembling balance. The last couplet of the same poem recalls the earlier love-lyrics in a similar manner:

124

> *And thence my ripe soul will I breath*
> *Warm into the Arms of Death.*

One can find many other passages in Crashaw's devotional verse to illustrate this practice. Crashaw does not, in passages like these, quote or borrow from earlier poetry; he does not ordinarily even suggest a particular passage or line from an earlier poet. Rather, by fleeting nuances of language, he suggests an anterior mode of poetic expression and hence of experience, and in a context which is new to it. More commonly than not, he suggests in this manner not what is most striking in an earlier body of poetry but what is most commonplace: an earlier poetic convention becomes the material of his perception, and contributes, along with other, apparently disparate, and non-literary material, the material of an extremely complex poetic structure. It is in ways such as this that Crashaw is traditional; he is experimental in the ways in which he pushes metaphor beyond the bounds of custom and frequently even of reason. Crashaw is noted for his experiments; the large amount of poetry in which the traditional predominates and the experimental is under full control is too seldom appreciated.

This illusion of simplicity, this retreat toward the norm, of which I have been speaking, can, however, be achieved only by those writers who have mastered the more emphatic and athletic exercises; it is inconceivable that a poet insensitive to the fresh and skillful enthusiasm of Sidney should achieve the subdued complexity of Crashaw, Jonson, or Herrick. The beauty of the later masters resides in a good measure in what they suggest and refrain from doing, not in that of which they are ignorant or incapable. Within the pattern of free verse, this kind of suggestion is impossible: to depart from a given movement is to abandon it; the absence of a metrical frame accounting for the agreement or variation of every syllable, heavy or light, and allowing immeasurable variation of accent, makes exact and subtle variation and suggestion impossible. Similarly, there is no manner in which the rhythms of a poem in free verse, such as H. D.'s *Orchard,* could be utilized or suggested in a poem in accentual-syllabic meter, for the two systems are unrelated and mutually destructive. In so far, however, as the difficulties of maintaining rhythm in new and structurally unsatisfactory patterns, may have forced poets and their readers to strain the attention upon certain fine shades of accent and quantity, it is possible that the free-verse poets may have eventually a beneficial effect upon poets writing in accentual-syllabic verse; in so far as free verse has encouraged careless substitution in the older meter, has encouraged an approximation of the movement of accentual-syllabic verse to that of purely accentual, its effect has quite perceptibly been undesirable. Eliot, Tate, and MacLeish exemplify the latter influence.

SECTION V: THE HEROIC COUPLET AND ITS RECENT RIVALS

A brief study of the heroic couplet and a comparison of the couplet with certain forms that have been used for more or less the same purposes as those which encouraged the couplet may throw a little more light on our subject.

The chief masters of the heroic couplet during the period in which it was the most widely used and the most widely useful poetic instrument are: Dryden, Pope, Gay, Johnson, and Churchill. In Goldsmith and in Crabbe alike the instrument is relaxed and the poem is diluted either with facile sentiment or with plodding exposition, although much admirable poetry may be found in these writers.

Dryden used the couplet for a wide variety of purposes. In his *Æneid,* it is an adequate epic instrument, only a little inferior to Milton's blank verse, the inferiority being so slight as to be fairly attributable to the men and not to their instruments. As an example of the grandeur to which Dryden is able to raise this form, we may turn to the descent of Æneas into Hell in the sixth book,

126

a passage quoted by Saintsbury, and as fine in its way as the original of Vergil.

Dryden employs the couplet as a powerful satirical instrument, as the meter for some of our greatest didactic poetry, and, in the opening lines of *Religio Laici,* as the medium for meditative lyricism of a very high order.

By changing to feminine rhymes, by placing the cesura regularly after the third foot, and by using an internal rhyme at this point in the first two lines, Dryden transforms the couplet into a song meter:

> *No, no poor suff'ring heart, no change endeavor;*
> *Choose to sustain the smart, rather than leave her:*
> *My ravished eyes behold such charms about her,*
> *I can die with her but not live without her;*
> *One tender sigh of hers to see me languish,*
> *Will more than pay the price of my past anguish.*
> *Beware, O cruel fair, how you smile on me;*
> *'Twas a kind look of yours that has undone me.*
>
> *Love has in store for me one happy minute.*
> *And she will end my pain who did begin it:*
> *Then no day void of bliss or pleasure leaving,*
> *Ages shall slide away without perceiving;*
> *Cupid shall guard the door, the more to please us,*
> *And keep out time and Death, when they would seize us.*
> *Time and Death shall depart, and say in flying,*
> *Love has found out a way to live by dying.*

The double meaning of the word *dying* and the compact wit recall slightly the Metaphysical school, as the former recalls also the song-books; the subject also recalls the song-books, and so does the careful suggestion of song-rhythm. Yet the poem has the sophisticated plainness of Herrick. These suggestions of earlier, simpler, and more emphatic modes are real, and they give a real

127

profundity to the poem, a profundity fixed in the pun on the last word. It is a profundity of feeling, not of thought. The poem is one of the best examples that I know of what can be accomplished by means of meticulous variations from a rigid norm.

Pope restricted the couplet more rigidly than did Dryden. In fact, Pope, and his friend and disciple, Gay, represent the closest approximation to what we now recognize as the normal form of the instrument. Earlier poets appear to be converging consciously toward Pope and Gay, who are, in turn, the norm from which later poets consciously and carefully depart. Pope in particular is crucial to the history of the form, partly by virtue of his very deficiencies.

Pope, for example, had no talent for purely lyrical composition: his efforts in that direction resulted in the genteel ineptitude of *A Dying Christian to His Soul, Eloisa to Abelard,* and the *Elegy to the Memory of an Unfortunate Lady.* But his inability so to express himself was compensated by, and may even have caused, a greater complexity of attitude and of subject matter in his satirical and didactic poems than Dryden ever achieved in any single work. This additional complication appears to be roughly of three sorts: the illustration of the general with a deeply personal allusion, such as occurs in the fine couplets on Gay in the *Epistle to Dr. Arbuthnot;* the intensification of the heroic aspect of the mock-heroic passage, till it takes on, as does the close of *The Dunciad,* a kind of metaphysical magnificence, an intensity of terror which renders the satire all the more savage and destructive; and the statement in language at once general, concentrated, dignified, and pathetic of a truth both tragic and so universal as to be wholly impersonal.

The first of these sources of complication, the introduction of the pathos of private loss or of self-justification, is roughly the subject matter of Churchill's greatest work, though Churchill's approach differs profoundly from that of Pope, and in exploring this particular field more fully than did Pope, Churchill in one

128

poem all but equals Pope's brilliance and range. The magnificence of the mock-heroic is to be found before Pope, in *MacFlecknoe*, especially in the passage which parodies Cowley's great description of the underwaters of the sea, which occurs near the opening of his *Davideis*, but the mock-heroic in Dryden is primarily in the interests of hilarity. Gay, in *The Birth of the Squire*, comes closer to Pope in this respect than does anyone else, but with this difference: Gay has wit but no malice, and almost invariably sympathizes with his victim and at moments appears wholly charmed by him, with the result that his pathos is humorous and specific rather than bare and universal. The last source of complication, or perhaps one should say the last mode in which Pope forces the didactic-satiric poem to invade lyrical territory, represents nearly the sole mode in which Johnson attains poetic greatness, and the mode in which Goldsmith achieved what is perhaps his only moment of great poetry.

I have illustrated the first and second of these classes by reference to familiar passages. Let me illustrate the last by quotation. Pope writes in *An Essay on Man:*

> *Heav'n forming each on other to depend,*
> *A master, or a servant, or a friend,*
> *Bids each on other for assistance call,*
> *Till one man's weakness grows the strength of all.*
> *Wants, frailties, passions, closer still ally*
> *The common int'rest, or endear the tie.*
> *To these we owe true friendship, love sincere,*
> *Each home-felt joy that life inherits here;*
> *Yet from the same we learn, in its decline,*
> *Those joys, those loves, those int'rests to resign;*
> *Taught half by Reason, half by mere decay,*
> *To welcome Death, and calmly pass away.*

It is this kind of pathos in isolation and perhaps more profoundly felt which renders memorable *The Vanity of Human Wishes*

129

and more particularly Johnson's two great prologues, to *Comus* and to *A Word to the Wise*. It is this kind of pathos to which Goldsmith builds in a few brief climactic passages in *The Deserted Village*, but especially in the following couplets, more famous, perhaps, in our own age for what may appear their democratic morality than for their rhetorical grandeur:

> *Ill fares the land, to hastening ills a prey,*
> *Where wealth accumulates and men decay;*
> *Princes and lords may flourish, or may fade;*
> *A breath can make them, as a breath has made;*
> *But a bold peasantry, their country's pride,*
> *When once destroyed can never be supplied.*

We might summarize these distinctions thus: Dryden touches successfully upon a wider range of experience than does Pope, and employs the couplet successfully in a greater variety of styles; but Pope through the concentration of his entire forces upon a single method achieves a greater range in certain individual poems than Dryden ever achieves in a single poem; Pope contains the germs of all the masters of the couplet to follow him in his century save Crabbe, and all of them save Crabbe achieve greatness by developing some one aspect of feeling to be found in Pope; Johnson, nevertheless, attains a greatness, even a universality, in a few poems, which appears scarcely inferior to Pope, chiefly by virtue of the way in which the dignity and grandeur of his character, his curious combination of private bitterness, public generosity, and Christian humility qualify his apprehension of relatively simple themes. It should be noted also, that if Dryden employs the couplet for a wide diversity of ends, by means of small variations, Pope, in combining a comparable diversity into a single complexity, varies the couplet noticeably less than does Dryden; yet he is successful, to the reader familiar with his sensibility he is one of the most exquisitely finished, as well as one of the most profoundly moving, poets in English. Churchill I reserve for detailed treatment. He is the most radical innovator in the history of the couplet, and by means of his innovations he uncovered a range of feeling, and created a poetry, as complex in their way, perhaps, as those of Pope, though he lived to master his discoveries in one poem only.

Churchill's early work contributes nothing of importance to the development of heroic verse: it is frequently good—the mannerisms described in *The Rosciad* are amusing, though little more —but it attempts nothing that Dryden had not already accomplished with greater brilliancy.

The Candidate, however, introduces a new procedure and a new quality of feeling into satirical verse, and the very structure of the poem forces one to study the innovation if one is not to remain, as a reader of it, suspended in ambiguity. The poem is directed against Lord Sandwich, who sought the High-stewardship of Cambridge, in spite of his notoriously licentious and unscholarly career. The poem, after various preliminaries, gives us a portrait of Lothario, a kind of ideal rake, whose identity is not given, but who is really Sandwich in disguise. At the conclusion of this portrait, the poet informs us that Nature, aghast at having created such a monster, by way of atonement gave us Sandwich, too. There follows a long account of Sandwich under his own name, an account which has at the outset all the appearance of the warmest eulogy; as one proceeds, one gradually begins to feel the undertone of irony, an undertone which becomes more and more evident, until, after several pages, Sandwich and his friends are being openly pilloried. This sort of thing, to the best of my knowledge, had never been done before; and to the best of my knowledge no one has ever pointed out that Churchill did it; Churchill, like Gascoigne at an earlier period and like Johnson in his own, was a great master obscured by history, that is, by the mummification, for purposes of immortal exhibition, of a current fashion—Gray and Collins, slighter poets in spite of all their virtues, were of the party that produced the

131

style of the next century and they have come to be regarded, for this reason, as the best poets of their period. We have not in *The Candidate* the mock-heroic convention of *MacFlecknoe* or of *Hudibras,* which, though it involves feigned praise, is frank burlesque. It is closer to a quality of Pope, to which I have already referred, but it is ironical rather than epigrammatical; it is more evasive, less didactic or illustrative of the general, more personal, closer to the sophisticated lyrical tradition of such writers as Gascoigne, Ben Jonson, and Donne. Churchill, in his ambiguous territory between irony and eulogy, awakened a number of feelings belonging neither to irony nor to eulogy, but capable of joining with both, and the most perfect example of the junction may be found in his greatest poem, the posthumous *Dedication to Warburton.* The poem opens thus:

> *Health to great Glo'ster!—from a man unknown,*
> *Who holds thy health as dearly as his own,*
> *Accept this greeting—nor let modest fear*
> *Call up one maiden blush—I mean not here*
> *To wound with flattery; 'tis a villain's art,*
> *And suits not with the frankness of my heart.*
> *Truth best becomes an orthodox divine,*
> *And, spite of Hell, that character is mine:*
> *To speak e'en bitter truths I cannot fear;*
> *But truth, my lord, is panegyric here.*
>
>   *Health to great Glo'ster!—nor, through love of ease,*
> *Which all priests love, let this address displease.*
> *I ask no favor, not one note I crave,*
> *And when this busy brain rests in the grave,*
> *(For till that time it never can have rest)*
> *I will not trouble you with one bequest.*
> *Some humbler friend, my mortal journey done,*
> *More near in blood, a nephew or a son,*

In that dread hour executor I'll leave,
For I, alas! have many to receive;
To give, but little.—To great Glo'ster health!
Nor let thy true and proper love of wealth
Here take a false alarm—in purse though poor,
In spirit I'm right proud, nor can endure
The mention of a bribe—thy pocket's free.

The feeling, and, as I have said, it is a new kind of feeling, is deeply involved in the rhythms, especially in the relationship of syntax to versification. The long and involved sentence, with its numerous parenthetical interruptions, hesitations, and after-thoughts, is foreign to the other masters of the couplet. It appears in Churchill's earlier work in a crude form, but here it carries as high a polish as anything in Pope. The style is more different from Dryden, Pope, Gay, or Johnson than they are from each other, and it is probably a more complex style than any one of them ever achieved, though all of them are sufficiently complex, Pope and Johnson especially so; Churchill does not, as did Dryden, vary the epigrammatic norm of the familiar couplet, but he established a different norm, from which he can, by means of suggestion, utilize the norm of Pope much as Dryden and Crashaw utilized the song-books, at the same time that he is engaged in arriving at a very different end. His poetry is one of profound and bitter innuendo.

The heroic couplet must have certain qualities which enable the poet employing it to pass easily from description, to lyricism, to didacticism, to satire, and so on, or even at times to combine several of these qualities at a single stroke. It is doubtful whether so much freedom is possible in blank verse; the only satirical poet who has employed blank verse with major success is Ben Jonson, and much of his satire depends upon significance derived from the structure of the play—the details from line to line are usually variations upon an anterior theme rather than autonomous sum-

133

maries. Ben Jonson himself employed the heroic couplet in some of his shorter poems, when he wished to indulge in a more direct and concentrated attack, and with remarkable vigor, in spite of the roughness of his versification. As a didactic instrument, blank verse is comparatively heavy and comparatively incapable of epigrammatic point; as a lyrical instrument, the range of blank verse, though wide, tends to be more closely limited to the grandiloquent and is less capable (in spite of charming passages in Fletcher and of *Tears Idle Tears*) of approaching the flexibility and variety of song. The heroic couplet, all things considered, appears to be the most flexible of forms: it can suggest by discreet imitation, the effects of nearly any other technique conceivable; it can contain all of these effects, if need be, in a single poem.

What, then, makes the couplet so flexible? The answer can be given briefly: its seeming inflexibility. That is, the identity of the line is stronger in rhymed verse than in unrhymed, because a bell is rung at the end of every second line; the identity of the line will be stronger in the couplet than in any other stanza because the couplet is the simplest and most obvious form of stanza possible. This mathematical and almost mechanical recurrence of line and stanza provides an obvious substructure and core of connotation over which poetic variations may move, from which they derive an exact identity. There is, in addition, a norm within the norm, at least in the case of every master save Churchill, the norm of the Popian couplet; and even Churchill can refer to this norm from a distance.

In spite of this regularity of basic scheme, there is no confinement of variation. The secondary rhythmic relationships of the couplet are unhampered by the rigidity of the primary, and the resultant set of relationships (the tertiary) between the constant element and the varying element, will be therefore unlimited, at the same time, however, that the constant element is providing a permanent point of reference, or feeling of cohesion, for the

134

whole. The poet may move in any direction whatever, and his movement will be almost automatically graduated by the metronomic undercurrent of regularity; and if he chooses at certain times to devote himself to prosaic explanation, the metronome and the Popian balance, emerging naked, are capable of giving his prose an incisiveness possible in no other form, and of maintaining the relationship of the didacticism to the rest of the poem —the relationship in regard to feeling, I mean, for a didactic passage would of necessity represent by explicit statement the rational relationships within the poem.

A longer stanza is likely to be tyrannical. Within a single Spenserian stanza, for example, one cannot gracefully abandon a thought and take up another, nor can one let a thought run over a large number of stanzas. In the couplet we may have an entirely free play of thought over a rigid metrical substructure; in the longer stanza, thought and stanzaic structure must, very largely, coincide. To state it otherwise, in the long stanza the varying and constant elements which have already been mentioned in connection with heroic verse tend to fuse in a single movement, which, if protracted, becomes monotonous; whereas the poet employing couplets and employing at the same time a sufficiently comprehensive plot or frame, could move at will through all the complexities of Churchill and through all the pure and isolated moods to be found in Dryden—it would be largely a matter of timing.

Such a form, it seems to me, is the desideratum of those poets, who, following more or less in the wake of Mr. Eliot, have endeavored to employ a more or less Websterian verse as a carry-all meter. Websterian verse is much looser than good free verse: by Websterian verse, I mean that kind of blank verse which has been so named in our time, the loose blank verse of the speeches of Bosola, of Mr. T. S. Eliot's Gerontion, and of Mr. Archibald MacLeish. In nearly all verse of this kind, the sense of the blank verse norm is feeble; the substitution of feet becomes meaning-

135

less because there is so much of it; there is no care for the distribution of secondary accents or lesser syllables; and there is no basic regularity which can be made to support didactic or other linking passages when they are necessary, for the Websterian poet simply does not dare to revert over the long distance to formal blank verse, for fear of destroying the cohesion of his poem.

This last weakness means that necessary connecting links are evaded, and the evasion has at least two consequences of its own: first, the poetry, in so far as it needs logical linking, tends to break down into lyrical fragments, as in *The Waste Land*,[1] and, second, the didacticism, not being properly accounted for, is likely to edge into passages where it does not belong, and in a fragmentary and unsatisfactory form, frequently in the evasive and indeterminable form which I have described at length in another essay under the name of pseudo-reference. This fragmentary didacticism is unsatisfactory, because the poems I have in mind—*The Waste Land,* and Allen Tate's *Causerie,*[2] and *Retroduction to American History* [3]—are fundamentally expository poems, akin to the expository poems of Pope and Dryden, in that they endeavor to give a summary of a contemporary view of life and a criticism of such a view.

To say that a poet is justified in employing a disintegrating form in order to express a feeling of disintegration, is merely a sophistical justification of bad poetry, akin to the Whitmanian notion that one must write loose and sprawling poetry to "express" the loose and sprawling American continent. In fact, all feeling, if one gives oneself (that is, one's form) up to it, is a way of disintegration; poetic form is by definition a means to arrest the disintegration and order the feeling; and in so far as

---

[1] *Poems 1909-25,* by T. S. Eliot, Faber and Gwyon, London.
[2] *Poems 1928-31,* by Allen Tate, Scribners, 1932.
[3] *Mr. Pope and Other Poems,* by Allen Tate, Minton Balch, N. Y., 1928.

136

any poetry tends toward the formless, it fails to be expressive of anything.

Mr. Tate's *Causerie* embodies social criticism and moral indignation, two traditionally didactic-satiric themes:

> *The essential wreckage of your age is different,*
> *The accident the same; the Annabella*
> *Of proper incest, no longer incestuous;*
> *In an age of abstract experience, fornication*
> *Is self-expression, adjunct to Christian euphoria,*
> *And whores become delinquents; delinquents, patients;*
> *Patients, wards of society. Whores, by that rule,*
> *Are precious.*

> *Was it for this that Lucius*
> *Became the ass of Thessaly? For this did Kyd*
> *Unlock the lion of passion on his stage?*
> *To litter a race of politic pimps? To glut*
> *The Capitol with the progeny of ostlers,*
> *Where now the antique courtesy of your myths*
> *Goes in to sleep under a still shadow?*

Compared to any modern satirical or ironical verse, the passage is vigorous; compared to the passage from Churchill, it wants finish. Yet it is in a sense more serious than Churchill, for it has wider implications and rests upon wider and more careful thought.

The poet who has made the most ambitious attempt of our century to create a carry-all form is Ezra Pound, but his free verse, though the best of it is better meter than any of the neo-Websterian verse, remains in spite of his efforts a lyrical instrument which is improperly used for other than lyrical effects.

As in all free verse, and as in Websterian verse, we have in Mr. Pound's verse no normal foot, nothing to take the place of the couplet's basic regularity, no substructure insisting steadily on

137

the identity of the poem, regardless of whither it wander. The meter, as in nearly all free verse, is wholly at one with the mood, and if the mood undergoes a marked change, the whole poem goes off with it and becomes incoherent. Purely didactic poetry is impossible in the form, because of the chanting, emotional quality of the rhythms, from which there is no escape, even momentarily: the rhythm implies a limited lyrical mood.

Unlike the Websterians, Mr. Pound in his best *Cantos* does not muddy his verse with secondary and uncontrolled didacticism: he is usually didactic, if at all, by implication only, but implication is inadequate, in the long run, as a didactic instrument. In the best *Cantos*,[1] at least, Mr. Pound is successful, whether in fragments or on the whole, but he presents merely a psychological progression or flux, the convention being sometimes that of wandering revery, sometimes that of wandering conversation. The range of such a convention is narrowly limited, not only as regards formulable content, but as regards feeling. The feelings attendant upon revery and amiable conversation tend to great similarity notwithstanding the subject matter, and they simply are not the most vigorous or important feelings of which the human being is capable.

The method, when employed in satirical portraiture, lacks the incisiveness of the eighteenth century masters:

> So we léft him at lást in Chiásso
> Alóng with the old wóman from Kánsas,
> * Sólid Kánsas, her dáughter had márried that Swíss
> Who képt the Buffét in Chiásso.
> Did it sháke her? It díd nót sháke her.
> She sát thére in the wáiting róom, sólid Kánsas,
> * Stíff as a cigár store Índian from the Bówery
> Súch as óne sáw in the níneties,
> First sód of bléeding Kánsas

---

[1] *A Draft of Thirty Cantos*, by Ezra Pound. Hours Press: Paris: 1932.

138

That had prodŭced this lígneous sŏlidness.
** If thóu wilt gŏ to Chiãsso wilt fínd that indestrŭctible
    fémale*
As if wäiting for the tráin to Topëḳa.

The passage is amusing in a way, but is soft and diffuse. Even *The Rosciad* affords more successful portraits. Notwithstanding the concreteness of the material, the meter is already outside the range in which it functions most effectively—the range, that is, of the fourth or of the seventh Canto. The meter is naturally elegiac, and the handling of it in such a passage as this is bound to be arbitrary and insensitive: the secondary accents fall accidentally, are hard to identify, and are neither perceptive nor intrinsically pleasing as sound, and so little attention is paid to shadings of quantity as to render the passage very awkward of movement. These defects in general are the defects of Mr. Pound's style, though in many passages they are far less evident than here. Like Swinburne, he has acquired an undeserved reputation for metrical mastery, largely as a result of a fairly suave manipulation of certain insistently recurring mannerisms, which, to the half-trained or the half-alert, appear signs of finish and control rather than what they are, the signs of a measure of incertitude and of insensitivity.

Mr. Pound has come no closer than Mr. Tate to creating a carry-all meter, but in his efforts he has sometimes created a purer poetry than has Mr. Tate while indulging in strictly similar efforts, chiefly, perhaps, because Mr. Pound has not been aware of comparably difficult material.

The Testament of Beauty, by Robert Bridges, offers one other experiment toward a carry-all form, which I should like, but am unable, to admire. The form is unrhymed duodecasyllabics, dependent for their existence as such upon a definite and reasonably workable system of elision, a form which Bridges calls syllabic hexameter or Alexandrin verse. The form, as I understand it, evolved roughly in this fashion: through Bridges' failure to recognize the principle of varying accent and the law of the identification of accent, as I gave them early in this essay, Bridges came to regard standard English verse as fundamentally syllabic, but hampered by certain other half-observed rules; the details of this notion he worked out in his metrical study entitled *Milton's Prosody*. In *Samson Agonistes,* he found certain twelve-syllable lines, which in nearly every case I should be inclined to read as violent aberrations from iambic pentameter, but which Bridges, since he had a predisposition in favor of the syllable-count as the basis of the measure, read as Alexandrins. On the basis of these violent and impassioned lines, lines whose metrical force, as far as I can feel them, resides in a terrible struggle with the iambic pentameter norm, a struggle comparable at moments to the struggle of Samson with the pillars, save that in this instance the pillars do not, I believe, quite yield, Bridges constructed an unrhymed syllabic hexameter, in which the accents follow no law save that of variation, and employed it in a long expository poem conceived, like most didactic poetry, at a low and calm level of feeling. The Miltonic struggle was eliminated, and had it remained it would have been highly improper in conjunction with the subject-matter; but so also was the Miltonic form eliminated. The meter suffers from one of the two basic defects of free verse: there is not, as there is in free verse, a limit to the variability of accent, but there is, as in free verse, no norm as the basis of variation, so that syllables within the line are loose and shuffling, though usually, by means of a little arbitrary classification one can scan the lines accentually. The result is a meter as invariably monotonous as that of Orm, and the reason for the monotony is the same: regardless whether one attempts to scan the line accentually, or whether one follows Bridges and scans it syllabically (by all odds the preferable procedure), it successfully avoids the accentual-syllabic, avoids, that is, any pattern or norm underlying every syllable, so that, though one has constant change

140

of movement from moment to moment, one has no variation, no precision of intention. It has certain advantages, possibly, for the purpose to which it is put in the *Testament of Beauty* over the heavily accented meter of Pound: its very monotony gives it a certain coherence, the coherence, however, merely of undefined intention, yet its freedom from the constant recurrence of the heavy measuring accent does not commit it so closely to a particular range of feeling; but if Pound's best *Cantos,* the first six or seven, are considered, the meter of Bridges is far less interesting in itself. This is curious, for Bridges, in general, is incomparably the better poet and the better metrist.

Bridges' syllabics, as employed by himself and by his daughter, Elizabeth Daryush, resemble free verse in certain other respects: they are more amenable to treatment if rhymed than if unrhymed, just as the double-accentual poems of Hopkins are firmer metrically than any of the unrhymed free verse of the Americans; and they are more likely to succeed in a short poem than in a long, for in the former the possibilities inherent in the various dispositions of accent can be more or less nearly exhausted without being repeated. Mrs. Daryush has been more successful, in my estimation, in writing syllabics, than was her father, though her greatest work, like that of her father, has been in the traditional meters. The following sonnet, entitled *Still-Life,* is one of her finest syllabic experiments:

> *Through the open French window the warm sun*
> *lights up the polished breakfast-table, laid*
> *round a bowl of crimson roses, for one—*
> *a service of Worcester porcelain, arrayed*
> *near it a melon, peaches, figs, small hot*
> *rolls in a napkin, fairy rack of toast,*
> *butter in ice, high silver coffee-pot,*
> *and, heaped on a salver, the morning's post.*

141

She comes over the lawn, the young heiress,
from her early walk in her garden-wood,
feeling that life's a table set to bless
her delicate desires with all that's good,

that even the unopened future lies
like a love-letter, full of sweet surprise.

One imagines that the medium could not be used with greater beauty than in this poem; there is certainly nothing in the work of the American masters of free verse to surpass it, and there is little to equal it. Yet like the best free verse, it lacks the final precision and power, the flexibility of suggestion, of the best work in accentual-syllabics, in which every syllable stands in relationship to a definite norm.

But I must now summarize my position in general terms. The sum total of the metrical virtues is necessary to didactic verse or to any sort of long poem, and is a profound advantage even to the shortest lyric. The sum total may be described briefly as follows: coherence of movement, variety of movement, and fine perceptivity. These virtues can occur in conjunction only in a system in which every detail is accounted for. That is, if the system is based (as English verse is normally based) on accent, then every syllable must be recognizably in or out of place whether stressed or not, and if out of place in a classifiable way; the degree of accent must vary perceptibly though immeasurably from a perceptible though immeasurable norm; quantity should be used consciously to qualify these conditions; in brief, the full sound-value of every syllable must be willed for a particular end, and must be precise in the attainment of that end. As language has other values than those of sound, this ideal will be always forced into some measure of compromise with the other values; nevertheless, the essence of art, I take it, is that no compromise should be very marked, and the perfection of art, though rare and difficult, is not unattainable. In a system such as English syllabics,

142

or as free verse, most or all of the individual syllables can have no definite relationship to the pattern; so that there is no exact basis for judging them, and they are, when chosen, relatively without meaning.

Traditional meter, then, like the other aspects of traditional convention which I have discussed in other essays, tends to exploit the full possibilities of language; experimental meter, like other aspects of experimental convention, is incomplete. To push the analogy farther, experimental conventions in general tend to abandon comprehensible motive, to resort to unguided feeling; similarly experimental meter loses the rational frame which alone gives its variations the precision of true perception. Or to put it another way: as traditional poetry in general aims to adjust feeling rightly to motive, it needs the most precise instrument possible for the rendering of feeling, and so far as meter is concerned, this instrument will be traditional meter. Further, as traditional poetry tends to enrich itself with past wisdom, with an acquired sense of what is just, so the traditional meters, owing to their very subtle adjustibility and suggestibility, are frequently very complex in their effects, whereas the looser meters tend to be over-emphatic and over-simple.

It will be seen that what I desire of a poem is a clear understanding of motive, and a just evaluation of feeling; the justice of the evaluation persisting even into the sound of the least important syllable. Such a poem is a perfect and complete act of the spirit; it calls upon the full life of the spirit; it is difficult of attainment, but I am aware of no good reason to be contented with less.

143

INDEX

145

146